# THE BUTCHER OF PUNTA CANA

LOUIS ROMANO

Published by Vecchia.



ISBN: 978-1-944906-28-3
Printed in the U.S.A. First Edition, 2019 Vecchia Publishing

## ALSO BY LOUIS ROMANO

*Detective Vic Gonnella Series*
INTERCESSION
YOU THINK I'M DEAD
JUSTIFIED

*Gino Ranno Mafia Series*
FISH FARM
BESA
GAME OF PAWNS
EXCLUSION: THE FIGHT FOR CHINATOWN

*Zip Code Series for Teens & Young Adults*
ZIP CODE

*Short Story & Poetry Series*
Anxiety's Nest
Anxiety's Cure
Before I Drop Dead (Things I Want to Tell You)

*Heritage Collection Series*
CARUSI: The Shame of Sicily

# Acknowledgments

I enjoyed writing this book and bringing Vic Gonnella and Raquel Ruiz back to print.

Many thanks to Jon Hill for his language skills while I was in the Dominican Republic researching this book. I could not have interviewed the women in this story without him.

Professor Clark Hill of Berkley College was a tremendous help with the information he gave me on serial killers and FBI profiling. His law enforcement background was shared with amazing stories and detail.

Special thanks to Kathleen Collins for her encouragement and chapter by chapter analysis.

Editing by Bridget Fuchsel was done quickly and with brilliance and excellence.

Always incredible thanks to my pre-readers. Your insight is invaluable.

And of course, no book is written without Rocco Sivage my 15 year old Jack Russell Terrier who has been at my feet for this and thirteen books.

# Dedication

This book is dedicated to all the fearless men and women who struggle and reach for a better life

and

to all the victims and the families of those who have recently perished in the beautiful land of the Domincan Republic.

May they all rest in peace and their families be comforted by the memories of their loved ones.

# CHAPTER 1

"Man, what a gorgeous day for the game. This place is golf heaven. Way better than Pebble Beach for my money," the driver of the golf cart said.

There wasn't a cloud in the bright, blue sky. White waves splashed the stunning sea's blue-green water against the natural coral and large, black boulders which abutted the golf course's emerald fairways and manicured greens.

The cart driver was one of four golfers from central New Jersey who were playing the ninth hole at the championship Punta Espada golf club in Punta Cana, Dominican Republic.

The foursome started their match at seven in the morning and were nearly at the turn by nine-fifteen.

On the ninth tee box, one of the golfers stepped up and placed his white ball on the tee. He stepped back behind the ball, surveying where he intended to place his shot. He took two practice swings before addressing the ball and making the shot. The middle-aged golfer took a slow back swing, but at the moment of contact, he dropped his left shoulder slightly. The result of his drive was disappointing, so he let out a word that made his buddies chuckle. The drive towered way left onto a waste bunker in front of a grayish coral cave, one of several similar caves that dotted the pristine golf course. There were two carts in the group, each carrying two golfers. Each cart was assigned a caddie, both dark Dominicans wearing white jumpsuits, baseball caps, and sneakers. The caddie who was on the errant shot, Tony, said he saw the ball land, and it was safe, meaning the ball was playable and not out of bounds.

One of the carts went toward their drives on the fairway, while the other headed to find the ball in the crushed coral waste area. The caddie for the errant shot followed on foot, as caddies were forbidden to hitch a ride on the back of the cart at Punta Espada.

"Not a cloud in the sky. Eighty-five degrees and a cool, steady breeze off the water. This is one of the few holes not actually alongside the sea. Spectacular!" the other golfer announced.

"Yeah, but by the time we finish, it will be so freakin' hot out here, it'll be unfit for this Jersey boy."

"I hear you, pal. That's why an early morning start is always smart here. No way I would start after seven, seven-thirty."

Their caddie ran a few yards in front of the golf cart, pointing toward the ball. As he predicted, it was in the waste area not far from the coral cave. The driver entered the cart onto the waste area, the sound of the crushed coral interrupting the quiet glide of riding on the perfectly maintained, lush, green fairway.

"I dink ju hab a gud shot to the green, my fren," the caddie announced. "One seventy-eight-shot." The tall, skinny, twenty-something caddie, with two, gold front teeth in his otherwise brilliant white smile handed a number 4 rescue club to his golfer.

"I was thinking about just laying up with a nine iron, Tony," the golfer offered.

"No, my fren…dis is jur bess club. Take a full swing an don dink about de groun. Finish high and ju will be berry happy, my fren," the caddie argued. His thick Dominican accent was understandable and charming. He really didn't speak English well, but his golf English was perfect.

The Jersey golfer went behind his ball to fix a target before taking his practice swing.

"Jesus Christ…what the fuck is that smell?" he blurted. The golfer gagged a few times before he walked away from the ball. As he moved ten or so yards from the cart, his partner, who was the driver, used the steering wheel for leverage as he pulled his large belly out of the cart.

"Holy shit, that's nasty. Smells like something crawled into that cave and died. Mother of Christ, that's bad." He, too, gagged a few times before upchucking some clumpy, watery vomit onto the crushed coral.

Tony, the caddie, took a green bandanna he had around his neck and fastened it over his mouth and nose. The other two players, who were ahead in the plush fairway waiting to hit their second shots, jumped back into their cart to drive over and investigate the commotion. Their caddie was already at the coral cave; he had also tied a handkerchief about his nose and mouth.

"Ay, Dios mio. Hay un cuerpo en la cueva. Hay moscas por donde quieras," the caddie shouted.

“What did he say? Give me that towel, will ya?” the heavyset golfer hollered. His partner handed him a green hand towel, which each golfer had in their golf cart. He poured a bottle of cold water over the towel and wrapped it around his face. Slowly, the golfer made his way into the cave. He stared in disbelief for a long ten seconds.

“Oh, my God. It’s a woman. She’s black and bloated and there are a million maggots and flies all over her. Holy fuck!” he announced. The other golfers, wanting to see the body with a macabre sense of curiosity, followed their buddy’s lead with their green towels.

Tony took out his cell phone, pounded on the numbers, then began yelling into it in ultra-rapid Dominican Spanish. He had the foresight to call the starter to describe the scene.

“Her pussy was chopped up and it looks as if her nipples were ripped off. Holy shit!” one of the golfers blurted.

“Can’t see her face, her head is covered by something!” another golfer shouted before he got a good whiff, losing his early morning buttered roll all over the front of the cave.

The clubhouse was very close. Several golf carts came screaming across the fairway toward the death scene. The club general manager, the caddie master, and the head greenskeeper were among the Punta Espada employees who raced to the horrific scene.

When the men all approached the cave, Jim McCabe, the general manager, quickly retreated from the horrific odor.

“Oh, my good God. Not another one!” McCabe exclaimed.

# CHAPTER 2

From his office on the 23rd floor at 26 Federal Plaza in New York City, FBI Assistant Director in Charge, Sean Lewandowski, opened his contact list on his desktop computer.

Lewandowski finally got the promotion he coveted for the past two years. GS 15 pay grade, $152,000 salary, corner wood-paneled office with a great view, two agents as his personal assistants, a seasoned secretary, and the entire FBI New York office at his beck and call. He always knew he could have done a lot better moneywise practicing law, but being in the FBI was his dream from when he was just a little boy.

Sean scrolled down to the number for his old friend, Vic Gonnella, and hit the call icon.

"Long lost! How is my big shot friend?" Gonnella asked. Sean's name came up in bold letters on Vic's cell.

The two hadn't talked since they worked together on the Boy in the Box cold case in Philadelphia three years prior.

"I'm glad you still answer your phone, pal. It's been too long," Lewandowski stated.

"Yeah, it has been. It seems time flies and life happens, even though we're both in the same damn city."

"How is my gal Raquel and the baby?"

"Raquel couldn't be better, and Gabriella, oh, she's not such a baby anymore! How is your family?

"Three kids now. My wife is Irish, so we're probably only half-done," Lewandowski laughed.

"Get a television, for Christ's sake."

"We miss you guys; we need to make a dinner date to catch up, but I didn't call for that."

"What's on your mind, Sean?"

"Our office got a call from the Director in Washington to refer you to the Minister of the Interior and Police of the Dominican Republic in Santo

Domingo. You know the old expression, shit runs downhill, right? So here goes. It seems the police in the Dominican are having a problem we have no jurisdiction over, and your name came up. It seems the DR may have a serial killer on their hands."

"Sure, I guess we are best known for chasing serial killers, even though it was only that one case like that we ever worked on."

"What do you hear from that character John Deegan these days?" Lewandowski queried.

"Nothing since he disappeared in Rome way back when," Vic fibbed. He said nothing about seeing Deegan in the Vatican when the entire College of Cardinals were almost gassed to death in the Sistine Chapel, or the fact that Deegan had made a trust fund for Vic and Raquel's daughter, Gabriella.

"Well, you'll be getting a video conference call at noon today from Minister Santiago Castillo. Of course, it's entirely up to you if you want to get involved."

"What do you know?"

"Not very much, except they think they have a serial on their hands and they are not equipped to deal with it. That's why they reached out to Washington."

"Okay, I'll cancel my lunch, and Raquel and I will take his call. I appreciate your call…I think!" Vic exclaimed.

"Thanks, Vic, let me know when you guys can break away one night."

# CHAPTER 3

Business had been very good for Centurion Associates. Since Vic Gonnella and Raquel Ruiz started their business, it grew to one of the largest private investigation and security firms in the world. The famous John Deegan killing spree case put Vic and Raquel on the international Who's Who list in law enforcement while making them both wealthy beyond their dreams.

Now it was time for them to pick and choose which major cases they would take on, and for them to grow their business at a comfortable twenty-five percent a year. Last year saw revenue of one hundred and twenty-three million dollars, breaking into the nine-figure world.

"I saw a seminar on YouTube today about businesses planning for their end game. We've never discussed our end game, honey," Raquel mentioned.

"I never thought of it. I just think things will happen as we get older. I dunno, maybe a big company will buy us. Then we take the chips off the table."

"Or leave it to Gabriella?"

"I can't even imagine her in this business. At least you and I started in the police department. I don't see her doing this at all. Gabby's already a wealthy girl, Raquel. Between our business and her trust fund from Deegan, she will be able to do whatever she wants."

"That Deegan thing bothers me. How can we accept a trust fund from a serial killer...really?" Raquel questioned.

"It's already all set up, honey. She gets millions in steps, starting when she turns twenty-five."

"When we were at the NYPD, we counted the years and worked on achieving rank for the best pension possible. Our daughter's life will be totally different. I never dreamed we or she would have all this, Vic."

"You? I thought I would retire and drive for some rich guy who needed security. We got awful lucky, didn't we?"

They went together to their conference room at 56th Street and Park Avenue in New York City. Three handpicked assistants and two field managers were already seated and waiting for a noon video call from Santo Domingo.

At ten past twelve, Vic was antsy and a bit pissed off.

"And we cancelled lunch at IL Tinello today for this bullshit!" Vic launched a Pentel pen across the room into a wastepaper basket. "Still got it!" Vic announced as the pen made its mark.

"Relax, Vic. They're on DR time. It's different down there. With the Dominicans, an appointment is just an estimate. You remember my family when we went to visit them in Puerto Rico? It's the same," Raquel laughed.

The ding of the intercom on the massive green and beige granite conference table broke the tension Vic brought to the room.

"Mr. Gonnella, Ms. Ruiz, I have Minister Castillo on the line. I will put him on the video screen now," a somewhat raspy, male voice announced. It was Jimmy Martin, a first-grade detective that Vic had worked with in the four-one precinct in the Bronx. Jimmy got his full pension and now worked for the firm. Jimmy got the strained voice from throat cancer surgery, attributed to his days working at the World Trade Center after 9/11.

The eighty-inch, black Sony screen at the far end of the conference room suddenly came to life. The bright colors on the screen filled the room with the waist up figure of a somewhat unhappy-looking older man. Castillo could also see Vic and Raquel on his screen. She, with her dark brown hair pulled tightly behind her head into a bun and her large brown eyes and olive skin tone, were perfectly accented by her rust-colored blouse. Vic wore a white golf shirt with a Shinnecock Hills logo, a three-day scruffy beard, and a bit of a scowl on his rugged face. Vic was a dweller. He was still ticked the minister was a few minutes late to the conference call. Raquel put her hand under the table to gently pinch Vic's leg to break his mood.

"Good morning, Minister Castillo. Buenos días. Do you prefer I translate from Spanish for Mr. Gonnella, or is English…" Raquel was interrupted by Castillo.

"Thank you, Ms. Ruiz, but English will make things a lot easier, I think."

Castillo's slight accent hinted that he had spent time in New York City. He was the only son of an uber-wealthy Dominican sugar cane family and had graduated from Columbia University Law School.

Santiago Castillo was a career politician in the Dominican Republic, clawing his way to the Minister of Interior and Police. At sixty-six years old, his dream of becoming president of his country was beginning to fade off into the multi-colored Dominican sunset.

Behind Castillo's cherubic, and a bit haggard face was a flag of the Dominican Republic on his left side and a round seal of the Ministerio De Interior Y Polícia with the words Dios Partia Libertad. God-Homeland-Freedom were scrolled vertically through a ribbon-like flag. The minister wore a dark blue suit, all three buttons fastened, with a sincere, blue and orange striped necktie. Vic was expecting to see a guy in a military uniform with a cascade of chest medals and a large, gordy hat. Castillo wore circular, wire-framed glasses which made his wide, round face and balding head look very large on the video screen.

"I want to thank you both for taking my urgent call today. I do apologize for being a few minutes late. We have had some technical difficulties in our telephone and video systems, it seems. At any rate, let me get quickly to the point," Castillo began.

Vic's mood changed for the better with the minister's recognition of not being on time.

Castillo continued, "Young Venezuelan women have been entering the Dominican Republic by the thousands. They come here to attract our considerable tourist trade for the purpose of prostitution. Unlike in the States, the oldest profession is basically legal here, not by legislation mind you, but we have accepted this trade in our culture. Of late, we have seen several girls murdered in the Punta Cana region, the jewel of our important tourist trade. Our economy can ill afford this publicity. Today, on one of the golf courses in that area, a third Venezuelan prostitute in a month was found murdered. The public is calling the killer The Butcher of Punta Cana, adding insult to injury." Castillo paused, waiting to hear from the other side.

"Minister Castillo, can you be a bit more specific about the murders? Any similarities?" Vic asked. His mood turned from sour to intent upon listening to the problem.

"Yes, Mr. Gonnella. Not to get into graphic details, I will leave that to my police department, but there are many similarities which point to the possibility that we have a serial killer on our hands. Quite frankly, my Ministry... my police are not equipped to do an adequate job in investigating and apprehending this kind of criminal, if indeed it even is a serial killer."

"Have any men been killed in the Punta Cana area recently?" Vic asked.

"None reported," Castillo replied.

"How can we be of help, Minister?" Raquel asked.

"I am prepared to invite you both to Punta Cana, all expenses paid, of course. Naturally, we are willing to pay for your time. We are hoping you can at least educate us as well as guide us toward the arrest of the killer or killers. To be very candid, this kind of news is not at all good for our tourist trade. We have already seen a slight reduction in visitors, and with today's news, who knows the damage that will befall us?"

Raquel and Vic both showed their poker faces.

"Minister Castillo, we are very sorry for your problems in Punta Cana and elsewhere in your beautiful country. For us to come down to assist you is a major undertaking for us, and it would force us to put many of our clients and other pressing investigations..." Raquel began.

"Ms. Ruiz, Mr. Gonnella, I implore you to help us. Just state your terms," Castillo interrupted.

"Well, we would need to discuss this, Minster Castillo, but we are looking at being there at least two to three weeks, perhaps longer," Vic stated.

Castillo interrupted again. Surely, he was not attempting to play poker or any other games.

"For fifteen days of your presence, we will wire your account five-hundred thousand dollars today. If you assist in the apprehension within that period of time, another five-hundred thousand will be sent. We are willing to put the second five-hundred in escrow. If it takes more time, we certainly can discuss your terms. We will have a private plane pick you up at the airport of your choice in the New York City area. You may bring up to nine people. If you need more, we can make further accommodations for that contingency as well. My people will fill you in on all travel and lodging plans. Trust me, you will be treated very well."

"I think those numbers will work, sir. I will have our attorney contact your people today, Minister Castillo. We will do our very best to help you catch this so-called Butcher of Punta Cana. We can arrive the day after tomorrow if all agreements are made today," Raquel blurted.

"My people will call you within thirty minutes. I look forward to seeing you both soon in Punta Cana. Thank you, and God bless you both."

# CHAPTER 4

"I'm a provider! Das what I do. I provide dings for people who live in or come to Punta Cana. If ju need a taxi, something fixed in jour house, some chicas, pot, a pizza, cigars, whatever. I provide services for people who are willing to pay. I been doing dis since I'm twelbe years old," Lenny proclaimed. "My reputation means eberything to me. If ju are happy with my services, ju tell others. And ju always will come back to see me."

Lenin "Lenny" Diaz was sitting at Mi Casa Lounge in the Bavaro section near Punta Cana. He was having a drink with three guys from Atlanta, Georgia who came to Punta Cana for some sun and some golf. At least, that's what they told their wives and girlfriends.

"Look, Lenny, you came very highly recommended by friends of ours back home. Well, damn it, you put us with these three chicas, and they did what they needed to do for us. No complaints there. We didn't haggle on the price, even though two hundred dollars for two hours seems stiff," one of the three yokels whined.

"Yeah, stiff...pardon the pun," yokel number two chimed in. He was more drunk than his buddies and a lot bigger. He must have been six-foot seven if he was an inch, with a crew cut, a red blotchy face, and a considerable beer belly.

"Those Venezuelan bitches robbed us! We took them back to our rental, they got us all drunk and happy, and while me and Jimmy over here were skinny dippin' in the pool with the girls, this other idiot was passed out drunk, and his chica went shopping in our rooms."

"That's some bullshit right there, Lenny," the big-gut guy bloviated. He stood up from the barstool for effect.

"And Lenny...they got my Rolex and about three hundred. They took about a grand from this fucker sittin' right next to you and two bottles of Vodka, and this guy's cellphone," the third knucklehead chimed in, pointing to the big guy.

"My friens. I'm so sorry dis chit happen. Let me go back and see what I can do for ju. I met ju here the other night, and ju guys are my frien now. Nobody does this to my frien. Listen, I will call ju later after I see these putas. Don't worry. I'm on the case for ju, my frien."

Lenny and the sloshed Atlanta crew quickly finished their drinks. The cab ride back to the rental house in Cocotal, was "provided" by Lenny, and he paid the driver.

Lenny was so furious, the veins in his now-reddened neck were bulging. His eyes darted back and forth like a wild animal. Lenny wasn't at all furious the Venezuelan girls he had hired had robbed his clients. He was enraged because he didn't get a taste of the loot.

The Venezuelan chicas all lived together not far from the Mi Casa Lounge, a block from Bavaro Beach. They chose to live in run-down, rented houses so more of their hard-earned money could be sent back to their families. Lenny parked his car not far from the apartment the ladies shared, and waited for a while to see the comings and goings. Lenny knew well that although prostitution is somewhat legal in the DR, pimping or running a brothel is not. Not that a few bucks to the police wouldn't make any accusation disappear, but Lenny was not interested in the hassle.

Just over six feet and, as the American girls would say, handsome-as-fuck, Lenny looked like he could be in an advertisement for Ralph Lauren. Shaved bald with huge, dark brown, mysterious eyes and a full, dark moustache, Lenny wore a white shirt that fell just above a tapered pair of white linen slacks. A pair of brown Italian loafers without socks gave Lenny a European-like look of sophistication and wealth.

Peering through a smudged and streaky window that had a flimsy, tattered, sheer curtain, Lenny could see one chica sleeping on a beat-up, drab, olive divan. Her name was Lilly. At twenty-four, she was one of the eldest of the three girls he routinely used for his clients. The girls each made a hundred American dollars per john, and Lenny pocketed whatever he could get over that amount. In this case, Lenny made a cool three hundred dollars from the Georgia yokels. That three hundred is the average monthly pay in the DR. On three hundred lousy dollars, most workers had two or three kids to feed on that measly amount, so Lenny did pretty well for himself on this one transaction.

Looking in every direction to see if he was being watched, Lenny went to the door that entered into the shabby apartment. The door was locked, but flimsy, and Lenny grabbed hold of the doorknob and hit his muscular shoulder into the door a few times until the lock snapped off.

Lilly never stirred. She worked long, late hours and needed sleep more than she needed food.

Lenny moved slowly over to the divan, unbuckling his linen pants as he went. He stood over Lilly, his pants and underwear now down by his ankles. Lilly's face was facing the torn, worn upholstery, her blonde hair flowing down onto the divan's seat. She was wearing a black bra and short, loose, white silk shorts.

Lenny grabbed his cock and squeezed it a few times as if he were masturbating. Suddenly, he began to urinate on the sleeping chica's head and shoulders. Lilly turned over, not understanding what was going on, as Lenny peed on her face. She tried to clear her eyes, and the piss ran into her mouth. She screamed and coughed out the streaming urine.

Lenny grabbed her hard around her neck, choking the unlucky young woman until her burning eyes were popping out of their sockets. He let up the pressure, putting his bald head near her face. He pulled his pants back up to his waist with his free hand.

"You motherfucking puta! You stole from my clients? My clients, and you offer me nothing? Now you will learn what I am all about."

Lenny began punching the wretched girl's face with his right hand until her nose broke and her front teeth were broken behind her braces. "You dare to defy me? You and your slut friends will pay me every penny you stole from those men. Where is the money? The watch? Where the fuck is it?" he screamed.

Lilly was sobbing, trying to see through her now cut and swollen, urine-soaked eyes.

"In the bedroom…in the closet," she blurted.

Lenny was not about to go into the bedroom and give the chica a chance to flee. He grabbed her by her hair, pulled her off the divan and onto the floor, dragging her along the tiled floor.

"Show me puta…show me!"

"In the shoes," she muttered. There was the Rolex, cellphone, and the money the girls had stolen from the Atlanta men, inside three shoes. The girls hadn't had the time to fence the hardware.

Lenny still had Lilly by the hair. He pulled her up onto the bed and threw her onto her back. He punched her face six more times, bringing his arm back almost past his shoulder with each horrific blow. Lilly's blood splattered all over the bed and wall.

He dropped his pants and flipped Lilly over. She was unconscious from the pummeling. He tore off her shorts in a rage.

Lenny wasn't done with her. He was fully erect from the excitement of beating the hapless young woman. He jammed himself into her anus, and after a few minutes, he dropped his load inside of her.

Before he left, Lenny wiped himself on her lace garment and dropped it onto her back.

Lenny looked down on his handwork. He was sweating profusely and spit on her back for the final insult.

"Puta…go back to Caracas, you cockroach."

Lenny left the apartment, calmly walking back to his car.

# CHAPTER 5

Punta Espada Golf Club posts a hole-by-hole description of their manicured golf course. Each hole is a golfer's dream. However, hole number nine had become the foursome from New Jersey's nightmare.

Hole 9 – Par 4 – With all the tees located on the top edge of the bluff and a virtual 360-degree view of the Punta Espada Golf Course and the Caribbean Sea, the adrenaline should be running high by now. A downhill tee shot will need to be struck well due to the wind, this dogleg left will play longer than its yardage shows. A series of three bunkers varying in size begin short of the landing area and extend midway to the green. It will be difficult to get up and down if a shot is hit into any of these bunkers. Position "A" off of the tee is protected by a large waste bunker along the left side of the fairway that begins at the landing area and extends up to the left side of the green complex.

Along with Jim McCabe, Fernando "Freddy" Reyes, the head greenskeeper at Punta Espada, arrived within minutes after Tony called the clubhouse to report the dead body. Freddy is among the most highly paid men working in the Dominican golf industry, and probably in the entire Caribbean. He demands excellence from his workers, who are paid well at four hundred dollars per month, a full one hundred dollars over the average monthly salary in the DR. He ensures the fairways are lush and perfectly manicured, the greens are fast and double rolled daily to maintain consistent ball speed on all eighteen holes, and he makes sure the sand bunkers are raked perfectly every morning, awaiting the golfers who expect a great golf experience. At three hundred and seventy-five dollars for a round of golf, no one walks away disappointed.

On the side, Freddy also owns one of the premier landscaping companies in Punta Cana, using his talents to maintain the grounds of the most beautiful villas and homes on the entire island.

"Everyone...please step back from the cave. The police have been summoned and are en route. I'm sorry, but no one is to leave the scene," McCabe announced.

"We were just playing the hole. I don't see any reason why we have to remain here," one of the Jersey golfers proclaimed.

"I'm very sorry, sir, however, the police have given me that command. You will have to be patient. We will give you a full refund, of course."

"Jesus Christ, and I was one under par!" another golfer blurted.

"C'mon Jeff, that's someone's daughter dead inside that cave. Show some respect, will ya?" the heavyset golfer proclaimed.

"Gentlemen, please move your carts onto the fairway and remain in the carts. We will send out plenty of water to you. Just sit tight," Freddy stated. Freddy is handsome, six-foot one with a perennial tan and wavy, dark hair. He somewhat resembles the famous Dominican-American baseball player Alec Rodriquez. Unlike most greenskeepers who wear denim jeans and cotton work shirts, Freddy wore pressed tan slacks, a tight white tee-shirt, and a light blue sports jacket. The only hint of being a man who worked in landscaping were Freddy's tan work boots, which were fully laced to the top and looked just brushed. He wore a white Panama hat with a slight tilt that nearly covered his right eye.

McCabe and Freddy peered into the cave but were backed up by the horrific odor of human decay and swarming flies. Like the golfers, McCabe nearly lost his breakfast. The two caddies sat in the shade of the golf carts, their baseball caps pulled low on their brows. There would be no tip for them today, money they had counted on to feed themselves and their families.

Piercing police sirens broke the serenity of Punta Espada, the Point of the Sword, named after a long strip of high, tree-covered land which jutted out into the sea.

Within minutes, four police cars were barreling down the fairway toward the scene. Freddy shook his head in disbelief at the sight of cars on his precious greenery.

As the police exited their cars, the distinct sound of a helicopter circled overhead looking for a landing spot.

Inside the Dominican police-operated Scout OH 58A 'copter was Lieutenant General Esteban Disla Martinez of the Identification and Investigation unit of the Ministry of Interior and Police. Martinez was in Punta Cana to lead the investigation of the prior two murders of Venezuelan prostitutes.

The helicopter landed fifty yards from the crime scene so as not to disturb the area with the wind from the large, whirling blades.

Martinez, with a thick cigar sticking from the middle of his mouth, headed toward the coral cave with three uniformed assistants in tow. His men called him Fumar for the twelve to fifteen cigars he smoked daily. Fumar also had movie star good looks. Tall and tanned in his blue uniform, studded with gold buttons and yellow epaulets with a blue and white braided shoulder strap finished by a military-like, blue-gray cap, with a yellow starburst on the black bill, gave Fumar a striking, no-nonsense image.

As he quickly approached the coral cave, Fumar began barking orders to his men and the hapless policemen milling around on the waste area.

"Jesus Christ, doesn't anyone know how to secure a murder scene? Where is the perimeter? The secondary perimeter? Look at this fucking place! Look at all the footprints around here! We couldn't find evidence with this mess. You all make me sick."

The two caddies had started to move back closer to the cave when the brass arrived, but were now regretting that decision.

Fumar moved toward the opening in the cave, covering his mouth and nose with his handkerchief.

He continued his rant. "What is this? What the hell is this? Vomit? Fresh vomit? Who was up this close? I swear to God in heaven, I will personally bust the man who threw up on my crime scene."

"General, it was one of the golfers who found the body who threw up," Tony the caddie blurted.

"Of course…the caddie knows everything, but you policemen are too busy looking to shake down someone for a few pesos. Miserable bastards!" Fumar seethed.

He continued. "I want only my assistants and the coroner, when he arrives, to be within thirty yards of that cave. I want a tent put up over on the fairway. Find a tent now! And a table and some chairs. Then I will personally interview the golfers and the caddies and everyone else that is here. Now you fuckers go and canvass every fucking home in the area and ask if they saw or heard anything unusual over the past few days. By the smell of the body, this didn't happen yesterday. We are pathetic. No wonder we have to bring in that fucking American."

# CHAPTER 6

"Look, mommy, look at the beautiful plane! Is that the one we're flying in?" Gabriella exclaimed.

"Yes, sweetheart, that's our plane. Just big enough, and cozy to fit all of us," Raquel answered.

The Cessna Citation X jet took off at nine in the morning from Teterboro airport in New Jersey, two days after Vic and Raquel had spoken with the Minister of Police of the Dominican Republic, Santiago Castillo. As promised, five hundred thousand U.S. dollars were wired into the Centurion Associates account, and an identical amount was wired to the company attorney's escrow account.

The agreement was clear. If Vic and Raquel's investigation led to the apprehension of the murderer or murderers responsible for the death of the Venezuelan girls, it would be a million-dollar payday.

Joining Vic and Raquel on the jet was their beautiful, seven-year-old daughter, Gabriella; a private tutor, Miss Theresa Panny; Raquel's mom, Olga; Jimmy Martin, the handsome salt-and-pepper former NYPD detective who worked with Vic in the Bronx Homicide division; and Jack Nagle, a highly decorated, combat-experienced Marine Captain and the company's director of operations. Nagle was in his early thirties, short, powerfully built, with a Marine crew cut and piercing blue eyes.

Minister Castillo hand-picked the Dominican pilot, co-pilot-navigator, and the stewardess, who would see to the safety and comfort of the seven VIP passengers.

As the plane neared the Punta Cana International airport, Miss Panny, who was sitting next to Gabriella, began her lessons on local history and geography.

"Look, Gabs! Look out your window and see the coastline of the Dominican Republic. See how beautiful and blue the water is. And all of the greenery and trees."

Gabriella tore her gaze away from the flashcards which had held her attention for the nearly three-hour flight. No iPad for this first-grader was allowed. Her large, green eyes peered through the window. The child smiled from ear to ear. A few of her front teeth were missing, with the beginning of her secondary teeth in view.

"That is really, really pretty, Miss Panny. Look, you can even see some white waves."

"Yes, it is pretty. This is the island where Christopher Columbus landed when he discovered the new world. It wasn't exactly here but he landed with three ships, east of Punta Cana. That was five hundred and twenty-seven years ago when some people still thought the earth was flat. It was a very important discovery for humankind."

"I've read about Columbus. He was Italian. My dad always brags about the Italians. We went to the Columbus Day parade, and my dad was marching with his police friends."

Gabriella looked across the aisle and smiled at her daddy. Vic was engrossed in some research on his lap top and didn't hear his daughter's quip about Columbus. She caught his eye and he winked and blew a kiss at his only daughter. He hadn't seen his sons in a while, which was heartbreaking to him, but their mother was always playing games, using the boys as ping pong balls to gain some economic advantage.

"Ladies and gentlemen, we will soon be landing in Punta Cana where the weather is a warm eighty-four degrees, and the sky is crystal clear. Please return your seats to their upright position, and keep your seat belts fastened until the plane comes to a full stop," the pilot announced.

"Ahhh, the sun! It beats twenty-eight degrees and snowy," Raquel declared.

"I don't think we will be spending too much time in the sun, honey," Vic stated.

"We will figure this case out in a few days, then we can spend a few days enjoying this gorgeous country. I plan to go back to New York brown like a chestnut."

"From your mouth to God's ears," Vic laughed.

The glimmering, oyster-white Cessna taxied to a secure area on the tarmac where several tan police vehicles, a shiny black Cadillac Escalade, and a phalanx of uniformed police awaited their VIP guests.

There would be no stopping and waiting on the immigration lines for the stamping of passports ritual, no x-ray of baggage, not even a walk through the quaint, thatched-roof airport.

The motorcade whisked the entourage for an eight-minute ride to a private villa called "The White House" in the exclusive Tortuga Bay community. The luggage was quickly removed by baggage handlers and police, using the official cars to transport their bags to the villa.

The caravan sped through the security gate in the fashionable development with the private, uniformed, armed guards saluting each vehicle as they passed.

"Reminds me of going to see the President at Camp David," Nagle said.

"When were you there?" Jimmy Martin asked.

"Obama was President. A Marine thing. I would have rather met Mariano Rivera."

"Hey, Mariano is Panamanian, this is the DR. You mean Sammy Sosa," Vic quipped. The three men laughed heartily.

The Escalade slowed and went left onto a large, circular driveway with dark orange paving tiles that matched the Spanish Colonial slate tiles on the roof. The front of the villa was all white, with stained-red, wooden window shutters. Four large, white columns jutted out from the enormous seven-bedroom, nine-bath estate. The grounds were impeccably manicured with a crisp, green lawn and virtually every flower endemic to the Dominican Republic. Reddish-orange Coralillo, majestic blue Isabel Segunda, deep purple Duranta, yellow Saman, and the bright yellow Bougainvillea flowers almost completely surrounded the entire property. Two large palm trees shaded part of the front yard, as well as a lush mango tree with its ripe, yellow fruit, waiting to be picked and placed on the breakfast table.

Waiting beneath a white canopy were an assembly of uniformed police brass, seemingly at attention waiting for the house guests.

A smiling lieutenant, General Esteban Disla Martinez, greeted Vic and Raquel as they alighted the vehicle first.

"Welcome to the Dominican Republic. I am Lieutenant General Martinez, at your service."

Vic gave Martinez a hearty handshake before introducing Raquel, their daughter, and Raquel's mom. All three exchanged pleasantries in Spanish with Martinez. Miss Panny and the two men stayed behind and away from the show.

Once inside, the entourage was greeted by Louisa, the cook and housekeeper, and Batista, the house boy. They greeted each of their guests with cold hand towels and a tray of fresh fruit punch. Louisa, a heavyset, dark Dominican, seemed very nervous, her eyes flittering all over the place. Raquel and Olga each hugged the woman and made some good-natured banter in Spanish. Louisa held both hands to her heart and smiled in relief. Batista, a twenty-year-old, handsome, jet-black Dominican, wore a dark blue Yankee baseball cap, no doubt to encourage tips.

A company of policemen followed into the villa with the baggage. Vic was busy marveling at the marble foyer and indoor circular tree and plant garden that separated the entranceway to the expansive living room. Gabriella and Miss Panny made their way directly to the large outdoor pool, which abutted the seventh hole of the La Cana golf course.

"Yay, what a great big pool!" Gabriella shouted.

"Perfect, we can have our swimming lessons right here," Miss Panny added.

"Leave the bags here until our guests get comfortable and decide which rooms they will take," Martinez barked at his men. Raquel caught his tone and was taken aback by his brash countenance and manner.

This guy with his chest full of medals and his fake smile and cigar breath is gonna be a problem, she thought to herself.

Martinez made another pronouncement. "Tomorrow morning, Minister Castillo will helicopter from Santo Domingo, here to Punta Cana to meet with you. You can relax from your trip today, and we can begin work tomorrow."

"We would much rather begin work after lunch and gather as many facts about the murders as we can. It's time that we begin a profile on the killer," Raquel countered.

"I see. As I am the lead investigator in the case, I can answer all of your questions, Ms. Ruiz," Martinez responded. His upper lip tightened a bit when he realized he was being told what to do by a woman.

“For now I will ask Louisa to show me the rest of this beautiful home, and then we can get started,” Raquel quipped.

# CHAPTER 7

"Okay, Lucy, tell me a little about yourself. What did you do in Venezuela?" Dr. Joel Fishman asked.

Fishman had lost his license to practice general dentistry and orthodontics in Boca Raton, Florida a year prior to opening up his current office in Punta Cana. That was ten years ago. The dentist had been accused of inappropriate behavior with some of his female patients back in the states.

"Well, where do I begin? I was born in the town of Maracay, where my father was an engineer for the county and my mama was a teacher. I was a good student and in my third year of engineering school when I decided I would rather eat than starve. Socialism is a nasty thing, believe me."

Lucy was twenty-two and stunning. Her sensuous, full lips and inviting, green eyes could make both men, and even some women, pant with desire. Her figure was nothing less than absolutely perfect. Lucy needed no fake boobs or other enhancements, as her body was all naturally sexy. Fishman was practically drooling on the young woman as she sat in his dental chair. His operatory was new, with all modern dentistry equipment imported from the states. No expense was spared, as his fees made his practice one of the most lucrative in the DR.

"I see. So no boyfriend or husband here, Lucy? No babies?"

Dr. Fishman was an unattractive man. Very short and too skinny, his Adam's apple jutted out about three inches. He wore a rust-colored toupee that tried, unsuccessfully, to cover his male pattern baldness. It sat atop his head looking like a small animal had crawled up there and died. Fishman had beady eyes, behind thick, horn-rimmed glasses, and a nasty case of halitosis. The bad breath was from a bad stomach, so at times, it was tolerable.

"None. I just do my job, pay my bills, and send what I can to my family," Lucy answered.

"What kind of bills can such a beautiful young woman like you have? No sponsor to help you?" Fishman leered.

"I don't have a sponsor. And no pimp. Just me and my friends and we get along just fine making money. Bills? My rent, some food, my cell phone, my hair and nails…" Lucy brushed back her long, light-reddish hair with a swirl of her head. "And then every month, I have to pay five hundred dollars to continue my visa. Only my first three months were free," Lucy added.

"Hmmm. You never know. Maybe I can help you with that visa bill. First let's get this work done and we can chat a bit afterwards."

Lucy wasn't sure what Fishman meant by help, but she suddenly wasn't completely comfortable with him.

Fishman slowly lowered the dental chair to a near reclining position, and moved the bright lights to shine on Lucy's face.

"Lucy, now just relax and breathe in deeply. In a minute, you will be in la la land. When you wake, you will no longer have any wisdom teeth," Joel Fishman whispered.

Fishman had started an intravenous sedative and administered nitrous oxide via a face mask.

"I feel a little funny, doctor," Lucy appealed.

"Just go with it, gorgeous. In thirty minutes, you won't remember a thing."

She didn't.

Unlike in the States, Fishman didn't need an assistant while attending to a woman. He tried that in Boca before a few of his clients blew the whistle on his sorry ass.

Lucy didn't remember or feel the extractions of her two mandibular third molars. Her orthodontist in Venezuela smartly did not attach her Invisaline braces to her wisdom teeth.

She also didn't feel or remember Dr. Fishman lowering the chair, putting is penis into her mouth, and cumming on her magnificent lips and pretty face. The deviate dentist would have eaten her out and fucked her, except Lucy's jeans were so tight, he had trouble getting them past her curvy hips. He gave up trying and just went for the low hanging fruit.

When Lucy came to, she was groggy and alone in the dental chair, the lights were off, and cotton gauze seemed to fill her mouth. She called out a pathetic, "Hola?"

"Yes, I'll be right there. I'm with another patient. Give me a few minutes," Fishman replied. He sounded as if he were out of breath.

What seemed to Lucy like an eternity later, Fishman walked into the operatory. He seemed a bit sweaty and in a rush. There would be no chat, as he mentioned.

"Okay, my dear…let me take that gauze out of your mouth. Don't put any more cotton or gauze in yourself. That can promote bleeding. The stitches will dissolve on their own. Take a few Ibuprofens for pain. You should be all right in a day or so. Your customers will never know the difference."

# CHAPTER 8

"General Martinez, with your permission, we would like to review the last several female murders with you, not only in the Punta Cana area, but the entire Dominican Republic," Vic offered. The meeting was held in the White House living room, with Vic, Raquel, Jimmy Martin, Jack Nagle, General Martinez, and two of his uniformed officers. They all sat at a sprawling white, sectional sofa that ran at least fifty feet throughout the room. All except for Martinez who sat in an oversized, white Havana chair, his black boots up on the matching white Ottoman.

Louisa had served a delightful Dominican lunch of baked chicken, black beans and rice, fried plantains, and a tossed salad. Olga made it clear to Louisa that no fried chicken fingers or grilled cheese sandwiches would be served to Gabriella. Her granddaughter would eat what the adults ate and not be given a choice like many kids these days. Miss Panny and Gabriella went to their adjoining rooms to unpack, and Olga went into her room for a nap.

Martinez seemed taken aback by Vic's request for a review of the murders. His facial expression betrayed annoyance.

"Mr. Gonnella, I…I'm sure that we will have the necessary research and information for you from our headquarters in La Capital. However, I can give you an overview of the last three murders here in Punta Cana."

Raquel took off on Martinez, deciding to bring her thoughts to a head and not play political games. "General, I'm sort of surprised this information has not been prepared for our arrival. Let me make some things clear to you. Our firm has been hired by your minister to perform a difficult task. We need cooperation to build a profile on whoever is killing these women. We will be looking at every shred of evidence that was collected at each murder site. We want to know every possible detail of the victims' lives. Commonality is one major aspect that we will be looking for. Were the women the same height, hair color, skin tone, and so on? Then, we want to do a detailed study of the photographs of the places the bodies were found. Were the women murdered where they were found or moved to the discovery site? How long were they dead? Were they left to be found intentionally? What similarities were found on the bodies? Their actual cause of death? We need to review the coroners' reports and autopsies, with the coroner, not just the reports. Have friends of the murdered women, other Venezuelan prostitutes, been interviewed? Do your police and detectives have any assumed suspects? We are looking for patterns, General Martinez. Perhaps the killer or killers have done this kind of crime elsewhere in the Dominican Republic. In short, General, we are looking for total cooperation from you and your department. If not, we will return tomorrow on your fancy private jet."

Vic didn't show any expression but was not surprised at Raquel's pounding of Martinez. Raquel had uttered her thoughts to Vic during lunch.

"This guy wants us here as much as you want the clap," Raquel had whispered to Vic.

"Ms. Ruiz, I assure you that all of the information and data will be presented to you tomorrow when my staff arrives with Minister Castillo. I was not prepared to review this today, and for that I apologize."

"So long as we understand one another, it will be best for the case and to stop whoever is murdering these girls," Raquel offered. She softened her tone just enough to send a polite peace offering.

"Ms. Ruiz, Mr. Gonnella...I think I need to clear the air prior to getting started on our mutual investigation. I must confess that I have had some resentment about your presence on this case. I have nearly forty years of service to my country, starting out in the military after college and then working my way up in the police department. I am not, thanks to God, a political appointee as so many others in our government are. I worked very hard for the position I now hold, and yes, I am embarrassed that outsiders have to be called in because we are ill-prepared to investigate a serial criminal. I often lose the perspective that the Dominican Republic is still a third world country in so many ways. With this confession out of the way, I offer you my total cooperation."

"General, it takes a great man to say what you just said. I admire you for your service to your country and for your honesty," Vic offered.

"Thank you, General Martinez. Now let's work together and find ourselves a murderer," Raquel smiled.

"Where do we start?" Martinez queried.

"Excellent! Let's turn this living-room into a war room. A headquarters, if you will allow the word. We will need more telephones in this place. At least six or eight. Two or three large white display boards; if possible, the ones you see on wheels. I'd like video conferencing capability. There is someone in Washington and maybe someone in Europe who we can tap for profiling ideas. We need interpreters for my men. Two shifts at least, and two video cameras for working in the field. Also, we are not sure who we are dealing with, so I want signal scramblers on all electronic devices in this place. No wiretapping and no hacking can be tolerated. Get your best computer people here, please. Let's get at least three desktop computers in here with high speed capability. If that's not possible, then set up laptops. Information is power. Lastly, I want twenty-four hour guards around this home, which I assume you have already ordered," Vic rambled.

"Yes, that was ordered by Minister Castillo. All of your other requirements will be here by tomorrow morning. Trust me, Mr. Gonnella, this is no small order in the Dominican, but I will move heaven and earth to have what you need," Martinez said.

"It's what we need, General. May I make a suggestion? My name is Vic, this is Raquel, that's Jimmy and Jack over there. Let's get informal. It's easier and less cumbersome. General?"

Martinez let out a belly laugh. "You may all call me what my men call me…Fumar."

"Fumar? Smoke?" Raquel.

"Yes, Raquel, I'm known for the many cigars I smoke each day, and right now I'm dying for one," Fumar blurted.

"Let's all go out to the pool. I expect you have enough cigars for all of us, Fumar?" Vic asked.

Fumar laughed again. "Of course I have plenty, but I must warn you. I only smoke Dominican cigars. Any Cuban smokes on this island are fakes…trust me on this."

# CHAPTER 9

At eleven o'clock the next morning, a helicopter carrying Minister Santiago Castillo landed on an open field in Tortuga Bay. Police cars whisked Castillo and several uniformed members of his staff to the White House.

Vic had been pacing the floors of the house since six that morning, watching a bevy of telephone and computer people setting up the requested hardware. Fumar did exactly what was asked of him and included a few items of his own. The general added a sophisticated copier/fax machine, along with portable bugging and GPS devices, should they be needed.

After the formal introduction of the minister, and pleasantries were concluded, everyone went into the living room, which was now morphed into Vic's requested war room.

"Very impressive, Mr. Gonnella. I see you have prepared us well for the task we have in front of us," Castillo pronounced.

"It was all made possible in a matter of hours by General Martinez," Vic replied.

Castillo gave a wry grin without looking at Martinez. The tension between Martinez and Minister Castillo was palpable. Castillo was from a well-to-do family who rose to his high level in the government because of political connections. Martinez, a kid from the slums of Boca Chica, broke his ass to get to his job.

They all sat around a make-shift conference table Martinez had also added to Vic's shopping list.

Castillo was shorter and heavier in person than on the video conference. His eyes were like two piercing brown buttons as he addressed his guests.

"Mr. Gonnella, Miss Ruiz, I'm certain you both know of the horrible and desperate conditions the country of Venezuela has been experiencing for the past several years. Whenever an economy collapses, the worst of it falls upon the people themselves. The Venezuelan people have seen their country fall from the eighth largest economic power in the world, to now experiencing almost eighty-five percent unemployment. Understand that the average monthly wage in Venezuela today is six dollars. The people are starving. There is no regular electrical power. Sanitary conditions are deplorable. Lives are being lost every day in Venezuela due to extremely poor medical care and street violence. So why am I telling you this?

Young Venezuelan women are entering the Dominican Republic as well as other countries for the purpose of prostitution, which as you are aware, is not really illegal here. We try to minimize the visas and the time these women can stay here, but other than banning them completely, which we have never done before, we find that thousands of these women are living in our country at the moment. Our tourist trade, as I mentioned to you in our first conversation, is a critically important part of our economy. To have a Jack the Ripper murderer in our midst, which he is now being called the Butcher of Punta Cana, is untenable. Frankly, many prostitutes who are Dominican citizens are already feeling an economic strain because of the Venezuelan competition. These Dominican women, our citizens, now find it difficult to make ends meet and feed their own families. As you can well understand, the poverty level here has become an even greater problem for us."

Castillo paused to take the pulse of Vic and Raquel.

"Have you indeed considered a ban?" Raquel asked.

"We have discussed it. However, from a humanitarian viewpoint, we realize that these women are sending back to their country much needed funds to feed their starving children and loved ones. How can we in good conscience keep them out? I think a similar debate is occurring in your country at the moment with a proposed southern wall abutting the Mexican border, yes?"

"Yes, indeed. Please continue," Vic uttered.

"The news of the killing of these prostitutes has already taken a toll on our tourist trade and we can ill afford to have this happen. You may recall, many years ago, a young American girl came up missing on the island of Aruba when she was there with a class trip. Her body was never found, and that publicity put a damper on Aruban vacations for quite some time. We need to stop this kind of publicity in our country.

"I'm embarrassed to say we do not have the knowledge on discovering and apprehending a serial killer in the Dominican Republic. This kind of thing just hasn't happened in our experience. That is why we need your assistance. Our president sends his sincere appreciation for your help."

Vic nodded politely to the minister, cleared his throat, and stood from his chair. He walked over to one of the large whiteboards. "Mr. Minister, gentlemen, we are all assuming the murderer is a serial killer. We need to determine if it is indeed a serial murderer, and we begin a profile as step one. We need to eliminate the possibility of a copycat killer, and that will be done through forensic evidence. Now so far, we believe there have been three questionable homicides. If it is indeed a serial, our experience tells us that three is a magic number. After three homicides, most serial killers take a respite, some time off if you will, before their next victim is selected. This may possibly buy us a bit of time. Mind you, this is not an exact science, so we can't be certain on this three-homicide pattern. I'm referring to statistics. For all we know, we can find another body today or tomorrow."

Raquel supported her husband's assertions. "We need to lay out the evidence you have gathered on each homicide and begin to form a profile on the killer. This profile will aid us to narrow down the suspect population and turn assumptions and speculation into apprehension."

Vic continued. "In my research, I found there was a Venezuelan prostitute murdered and beheaded last December in San Pedro de Macoris, a town which is not anywhere near Punta Cana. Can anyone tell me the circumstances behind this homicide? I am interested in knowing about this particular homicide and any other killings of Venezuelan prostitutes in the Dominican Republic over the past few years. We are looking for commonality and potential copycat activity. It may lead us nowhere, but it's a good starting point."

"I worked that case," one of the minister's staff declared. José Luis Vasquez, a captain in the national police, dark skinned in a camouflage uniform and black beret, stood at his place. Vasquez spoke no English. One of the interpreters was immediately called into the meeting.

"Captain Vasquez, please be detailed in your report," Fumar ordered.

"That victim was a twenty-eight-year-old Venezuelan prostitute from the Caracas area. Keila Andrea Pernia Alvares was her name. She was in the Dominican Republic for three days. Her body was found in a river in San Pedro de Macoris. Her body was thrown from a bridge by her assailant. Her head was severed and found separately from her body. The autopsy showed the cause of death to be strangulation. Her passport and driver's license was found on her person. She met her assailant in Boca Chica, some forty kilometers from where her body was discovered. Her murderer was an American tourist who admitted the killing under interrogation."

"Captain Vasquez, can you describe the victim?" Vic asked.

"I have brought along an old photograph anticipating your questions. I also have the official reports as well as the autopsy report," Vasquez added.

"May we see the photo and the reports, please?" Vic requested.

Vasquez passed the young woman's file to Vic. Raquel, who was sitting next to Vic, shared the view of the file.

Keila was a beautiful, light-skinned woman with shoulder length, chestnut-brown hair, brown, almond-shaped eyes, prominent brown eyebrows, full lips, and a pleasant smile. Her smile did not expose her teeth.

"The distance from Boca Chica to San Pedro de Marcoris is about thirty minutes by car?" Raquel asked.

"Yes ma'am."

"Was the murder done in Boca Chica?"

"No. The perpetrator admitted to killing the victim in his car near the river."

"Did he give a motive under interrogation?" Raquel queried.

"Yes, he did. He said he fell in love with her and wanted her to stop being a prostitute."

"So, is it your opinion and the opinion of the ministry that this was a one-off?" Vic asked.

"I am sorry, but I am not familiar with this term," Vasquez responded.

"Sorry, was this his only homicide? Did he murder any others?"

"No other women were discovered murdered in that zone. He only admitted to killing the victim. He blamed it on love."

"Did he admit to the decapitation?" Vic followed.

"He did, sir."

“Was there any body mutilation?” Raquel asked.

“None,” Vasquez replied

“My next question is to all assembled. Were any of the bodies recently found in Punta Cana decapitated?”

“No, they were not. However, each victims head was covered. All three had sexual mutilation,” Fumar advised.

“Covered? What were they covered with, General?”

“Burlap, Ms. Ruiz. Their heads were all covered in burlap.”

# CHAPTER 10

Louisa served strong Dominican Coffee with warm milk to the group at the makeshift conference table. Promptly at one, a lunch of ham sandwiches and homemade guacamole and chips was offered while everyone worked.

"I would like to see on a map where the bodies were found. I'm also interested in knowing the proximity of each site from one another," Vic articulated.

Fumar chomped on an unlit Arturo Fuente Churchill cigar. He was dying to put a light to it but wouldn't dare smoke inside such a beautiful home.

"We have brought along a map of the area," Fumar replied. The general looked at one of his men who quickly retrieved the zone map from his attaché and attached it to one of the whiteboards. The map had three prominent Xs in the locations, symbolizing where the three women's bodies were found.

Fumar stood next to the board, using his cigar as a pointer.

"This is where the last body was found. This is on the ninth hole of the Punta Espada Golf Club. She was found in a shallow coral cave on the fairway."

"How long do you estimate the body was there?" Raquel asked.

"Some golfers accidentally found the body. The odor of decomposition attracted their attention. The girl was found on Monday morning. The coroner's report, which is in the folder you both were given, indicated the body was moved to this location on the prior Friday. Time of death was approximated to that past Friday evening."

"So how do we know the body was moved there?" Raquel queried.

Vic chimed in, "Excellent question, Raquel. Was the body carried, dragged, or driven to the spot?"

"...and no one noticed this kind of activity?" Raquel followed.

Fumar replied, "There was no sign of struggle on the sand in the waste area. The body was found with her arms neatly folded over her chest. As you will see, the body was mutilated. There was no blood found in or around the cave. The girl's body was likely moved in the dark. There is no lighting near that location. Photographs are in your folders."

"Okay, so we know there was sexual mutilation, done on a Friday, body was moved to the cave, so the homicide was committed elsewhere. How did the assailant move the body across the fairway, or down the waste area, and into the cave?" Raquel followed.

"Here is where I will be embarrassed by my response to you. The crime scene was totally contaminated. We are assuming some kind of vehicle was used by the killer. However, with all of the pandemonium that followed the discovery from the four golfers and two caddies and Punta Espada management, any relevant tire marks on the fairway and crushed coral were disturbed. Frankly, if there were tracks on the stone, and the body was found on Monday, the grounds crew likely would have raked the waste area at least once, if not three times. According to the head greenskeeper, it is his practice to have the waste bunkers raked with a vehicle that pulls a mesh mat every morning."

"I see. Can you please provide us with the names of everyone who was at the scene that day? You know...management, maintenance, golfers, police, caddies," Raquel queried.

"Yes, Ms. Ruiz. I realize that in your mind, as it should be, everyone is a suspect," Fumar replied.

Raquel smiled politely.

"Tell us about the mutilation, please. I know we can get the medical report, but I want to hear it from your perspective," Vic asked.

Fumar nodded at another officer in his group. Lieutenant Mateo Castillo was a short, robust, mid-thirty career member of the national police who lived with his parents in Santo Domingo. He was single and married to his job. Vic and Raquel noticed a familiarity with Minister Santiago Castillo. Neither asked if the older Santiago and Mateo were related. Turns out that Mateo is the minister's nephew. This is how things are in the DR. Nepotism is a way of life.

Mateo seemed overbearing just by his look and manner. He was the kind of officer that any of his men would like to punch square in his face. However, he was well prepared for his meeting with the Americans.

“Lady and gentlemen. Our first victim, Samantha Franco, turned twenty-five years old three days before her death. She was in the Dominican Republic just five days. She had been in the Venezuelan military for three years and then worked odd jobs. There are indications she was a prostitute for a short while in her country. Her father is a military policeman, and her mother is a police officer. The victim’s body was found buried under some leaves and branches in the Indigenous Eyes Ecological Park near the Punta Cana Resort and Hotel. This X marks the exact spot where Samantha was found. Her body was similarly mutilated. Her breast nipples were removed by what seems like a serrated knife. Her vagina…was badly damaged,” Mateo seemed embarrassed by Raquel’s presence when speaking about the murdered girl’s private parts. A hint of red rode up on his neck to his hairline.

“Lieutenant Castillo, please tell us more about the park where she was found,” Vic asked.

“Yes, sir. It is an ecological reserve with winding, walking dirt paths throughout the park. It is made to look like a subtropical rainforest. The reserve is a park for families and honeymooners who want to stroll among the lagoons and hope to see an iguana.”

“When does the park open and close, or is it just an open area?” Raquel queried.

“No, madam. The park requires an entrance fee and is open every day from sunup to sundown. At times, young people are chased from the park after hours.”

“And why are they in the park after hours, Lieutenant? Oh… I’m sorry... I retract that question. I just realized…sorry,” Raquel stuttered. It was Raquel’s turn to turn red.

Vic chuckled and looked at Raquel, giving his woman a wink.

“Now, Lieutenant, tell me, you said lagoons. Describe them please.”

“Yes, sir, within the fifteen-hundred acres of the sanctuary, there are twelve crystal clear lagoons, five of which can be used for swimming by the paying public. The Taino Indians, the pre-Columbian inhabitants of our country, called the lagoons “eyes.” Therefore, the name of the park. Indigenous Eyes,” Mateo lectured.

Minister Castillo cleared his throat and spoke for the first time in the meeting. "It seems to me that Lieutenant Castillo may have made an excellent tour guide…or archeologist." The minister did not seem pleased.

"No, no, forgive me, Minister Castillo, but as many details as possible are needed. This is why we want to fully understand the locations where the bodies were found. Now, Lieutenant Castillo, please tell me about these lagoons. How close to the lagoon was the deceased found?" Vic inquired.

"Yes, sir. She was found in some underbrush right next to the first lagoon in the park. Perhaps thirty meters inside the park."

"So why do you think the killer didn't just drop her body into the lagoon?" Raquel asked.

"Madam, the lagoon is crystal clear and a depth of maybe thirty or forty meters. She would have been found as easily in the water as she was just alongside the walking path. Samantha's body was in no way hidden."

"Ah, so like the body at Punta Espada, the killer wanted his handiwork to be found easily."

"Yes, sir. That is my belief and my contention," Lieutenant Castillo sprouted. His eyes quickly moved to and away from his scowling uncle.

Before any further questions were asked, Minister Castillo stood to speak. "Gentleman, I must excuse myself. I am due back in La Capital to meet with our President. He is anxious to hear of the movement on this case, as well as some other pressing matters I must attend to. Mr. Gonnella, Ms. Ruiz, please, I am at your service. My aide will give you my personal cell and home numbers, should you need to reach me at any time."

All of the members of the police departments stood at attention while Vic and Raquel shook the Minister's hand. He was gone in a politician's flash.

Raquel excused herself for a moment to greet Gabriella, Olga, and Ms. Panny as they were heading to the pool.

"I suggest we take a break for a cigar and more discussion outside under the tiki hut," Fumar blurted.

"That's some tiki hut. It's bigger than my fucking house," Jimmy Martin whispered to Nagle.

“At the risk of causing an international incident, Fumar…may I offer you a Rocky Patel Nicaraguan?” Vic joked.

“Vic, I would smoke a rope at this point,” Fumar laughed.

# CHAPTER 11

While Vic, Raquel, Jimmy Martin, and Jack Nagle had cigars and chatted with Fumar and his men under the tiki hut, Miss Panny gave Gabriella her swimming lesson. Olga relaxed on a chaise lounge watching her only grandchild with the eyes of a hawk. Olga wasn't a strong swimmer and didn't love the water.

Miss Panny, at twenty-seven years old, always dressed conservatively when she tutored the children of her wealthy clients or taught kids who were in the acting world and were required by the Screen Actors Guild to study on set. Underneath the unadventurous garb, Miss Panny had a smoking hot body and gorgeous dancer's legs. With her light brown hair pulled back into a bun and a form fitting, blue, one-piece bathing suit, she caught the eyes of Fumar's men. Lieutenant Castillo was especially distracted from the conversation about the murdered victim who had not yet been discussed.

Raquel and the men made their way back to the war room. Castillo tried to make eye contact with the young teacher to no avail. Miss Panny was laser focused on her charge.

At every seat, Louisa had placed a small dish of mango, apples, grapes, and pineapple. No one made a move toward the refreshing dessert.

"Let's hear about the first homicide," Vic requested.

"Sergeant Lopez will provide any information we need," Fumar announced.

The youngest of the aides, Manuel Lopez, was only twenty-eight years old and considered an up-and-comer in the national police. He had worked himself up the ranks and tested the highest in the department to be appointed as sergeant. A big plus for Lopez was that his father was a prominent attorney in Santo Domingo and a major political supporter and advisor of the President of the Dominican Republic.

Lopez looked like a striking six-foot poster boy for the Ministry of Interior and Police in his perfectly fitted uniform, beaming white smile, and wavy black hair. The sergeant had an air of sophistication that was more inborn than taught.

"Carla Cisneros' body was found on the beach within walking distance from this villa. She was lying in a beach chair, facing the water, her body covered with white towels. Her face was also covered with a towel, but under the towel, her head was covered with burlap. The assailant left the wire ligature with which he choked her to death. The autopsy confirmed the cause of death to be asphyxiation. Like the other two victims, her breasts and genitalia were mutilated. You may view the autopsy reports and other information in the folder I prepared for you," Lopez offered.

"How long was the victim left on the beach? Was there evidence she was killed where she was found?" Raquel asked.

"Her body was found on the first Saturday of the month by a uniformed private guard, just after sunrise. Her body temperature and rigor mortis indicated she was murdered the night before at approximately one o'clock in the morning. Her body was not in full rigor by the time the coroner arrived, which was about eight a.m. There was no blood in the sand, no signs of a struggle. There were tire marks around the beach chair."

"What kind of tire marks?" Raquel countered.

"You will see photos of the markings in your file. Basically, they were golf cart-like tires but different than the golf carts which are used at the courses here. Our investigation continues on those tracks."

"The absence of blood..." Lopez continued. Raquel stopped him.

"Sergeant, let's stay on the tire marks. Were plaster impressions made of these tracks?"

"No, Ms. Ruiz. I'm sorry to say that was overlooked."

Fumar moved uncomfortably in his chair.

"So the photos are all we have. Okay, were these pictures blown up to examine the tread and manufacturer?" Raquel queried.

"To my knowledge, that has not been done."

"Okay, Jimmy, will you get on that right away?" Raquel ordered. Raquel fought the impulse to shake her head in disbelief.

"Done," Jimmy Martin replied.

Carla Cisneros arrived in the Dominican Republic from Caracas on a Monday. By Friday, she was dead. Conviasa Airline allowed her body to be flown back to her country using her four hundred and seventy-three-dollar, round trip ticket.

Her killer texted her cellphone number the afternoon of her death.

"Hello, Carla. A friend told me about you and how beautiful you are. I would like to meet you tonight. Are you available?"

"Yes, mi amor. What time?"

"Nine o'clock?"

"I am free from nine to eleven."

"Perfect. Can we meet at the Supermercado Nacional store near Punta Cana airport?"

"I can take a taxi from Bavaro. I expect to be reimbursed to and from."

"Not a problem. What is your fee for the two hours?"

"Two hundred American dollars, plus tip, plus taxi," Carla responded.

"That is a bit more than normal, but you will see that I am quite well off. Perhaps we can negotiate for some extras?"

"Like what?"

"Anal licking?"

"That will be more, of course."

"That is fine. I will pay extra."

"I take half the money up front."

"No problem, Carla."

"Okay, mi amor. Nine o'clock at the Nacional then."

"Nine, sharp!"

"Okay. TTYL."

Nine o'clock sharp in the Dominican means be there on time. Simply nine o'clock could mean anywhere from nine to ten thirty. Carla was on time.

Carla exited the taxi at five minutes before nine. A new SUV in the food store's parking lot flashed its lights a few seconds later. Carla waved and made her way to the passenger door.

"You are every bit as beautiful as my friend said. Even more so," the killer blurted.

"Thank you. You are good looking, too."

Carla was dressed in skinny jeans. Her butt was perfect in these pants. Her three-inch high-heels and skimpy red halter top exposed a rock-hard midriff. Carla's cleavage was perfect, the tops of her ample, silicone enhanced breasts seemed to explode outside the top.

"My home is not very far. I think you will be quite impressed."

"Okay, mi amor. How far is it?"

"Ten minutes. If you like, you can stay the night."

"We shall see. But then the fee is much more than we discussed," Carla negotiated.

"You're right. Let's see."

They chatted about the great weather and the full moon as they drove the ten minutes up to a spectacular villa with a circular driveway. Impressive lighting dramatically shadowed the gardens, the palm trees, and twelve, magnificent brown pillars in the front of the brown and beige brick estate.

"My house is your house. Relax and enjoy yourself. We can use the pool later if you like."

"I just had my hair done so I'm not sure about getting it wet."

"As you wish, beautiful. Let's have a nice drink first. What would you like?"

"Presidente beer, please."

"Okay, I will have the same. Fancy a shot of Brugal SV?"

"Why not?"

They sat on a leather sofa as the killer poured the beer into a frosted glass, then poured a double shot of the Dominican rum into a pony glass, neat. Carla took out her cellphone and took a few photos of the gorgeous living room.

Carla downed the shot in two gulps and followed with a pull of the Presidente.

"Here, take a piece of fresh coconut with me. It's very refreshing."

"My favorite," Carla replied as she chewed on the soft meat of the coconut.

"Your breasts are lovely. May I feel them?"

"Of course. You paid for them, mi amor."

A gentle squeeze then a soft kiss to Carla's cleavage did nothing to excite the chica.

The killer got up from the sofa and went to the entertainment center, putting on a romantic Cuban CD.

The murderer gently removed Carla's pants and thong, tossing them aside before going down gently on the pretty Venezuelan. Carla enjoyed the action, placing one leg on the assailant's shoulder. The licking stopped before the chica could get really into it.

"You are Cuban?" Carla queried.

"One hundred percent."

"My grandmother was born in Cuba."

The killer stared into Carla's big brown eyes with a quizzical look.

"What is it, mi amor?" Carla asked.

"Nothing…just waiting."

"Waiting? For what?"

Suddenly, Carla's head began to spin. Thinking it was the Brugal, she shook her head to kick away the cobwebs. The dizziness worsened.

"I feel funny. What did you give me?"

"Not to worry, Carla. Soon you will feel like sleeping."

"I want to leave…I want to…"

As the young Venezuelan tried to stand, her body slumped back into the sofa. The assailant stepped around the sofa behind the hapless girl. A wire garrote was gently placed around Carla's pretty soft neck.

"Now you will pay, you fucking bitch. You slut!"

Carla knew what was about to happen as the pressure on her neck began to choke her.

"Please don't...please I have a baby...please."

"Fuck you and your baby. You think you can come here and..."

The young woman choked and tried to scream to no avail. Her eyes began to pop out of their sockets as she choked out her last words, "Please...why?"

In a few minutes, the girls lifeless body was on the polished wood floor of the living room.

"There you are, pretty one. You can join your friends in hell, you slut."

The assailant dragged the body outside to a grassy area beside the pool. Carla's top was removed and thrown aside. The killer took a serrated knife and nearly carved out the girl's fake breasts. Then the knife did its job on the ill-fated young woman. Very little blood was spilled onto the grass before Carla's face was covered in a small burlap sack.

The murderer brought a four-seat golf cart to the body, pulling the chica's body onto the back seat.

"This nice watch is for me. A souvenir of our time together," the murderer added before driving off into the night.

"Sergeant, how was the victim identified, and please describe her looks for us," Vic asked.

"Miss Cisneros' purse was found intact under the beach chair. The only fingerprints that were found on the bag were her own. Her identification was also intact. She had several thousand pesos in her bag. The only thing that seemed missing was her watch. A tan line on her wrist indicated she wore a watch. It was not a very expensive watch according to her friends. I don't recall the model, but that information is in the report. I'm sorry, I do remember now, my ex-wife has one. It was a Swatch. Sorry. One more thing, if she had a cell phone, it wasn't found on or near her body."

"Okay, and what were her features, please?" Vic asked.

"She was a very pretty girl. Brown hair, shoulder length. She had brown eyes, her eyebrows had just recently been weaved. They were thick and brown like her hair. Her nails were manicured. She had braces on her teeth."

"Thanks, Sergeant Lopez," Vic offered.

Fumar took an unlit cigar from his mouth and placed it on the corner of the conference table. He reached for the fresh fruit that was in front of him.

"Everyone, please enjoy this wonderful treat," Fumar said.

Only Lieutenant Castillo did not reach for the compote.

"Gentlemen, I think tomorrow morning we will begin to put down the similarities of each homicide on the board. This is how we will help determine the profile and begin to build our suspects. Right now, I would like to take a ride to see all of the locations where the bodies were found. From the look of the map, they seem to be no more than five or six miles from one another. I can't convert that into kilometers so fast," Vic chuckled.

"Nine or ten kilometers, sir," Lieutenant Castillo jumped in.

"Thank you. Classic serial killer M.O. We will review that first thing tomorrow."

"Vic, just one thing I want to discuss before we adjourn before dinner. There are many common elements that I see already and some that were not yet mentioned. I want to study the autopsy reports tonight. The one most obvious thing to me is the burlap covering on all the victims. I would like for everyone to think about what common uses for burlap is here in the DR. And get samples of burlap to test against what was found on the victims," Raquel stated.

"Good idea," Vic replied. He looked at Raquel with admiration.

"I suggest we meet at seven-thirty tomorrow morning. I will ask Louisa to have breakfast ready for all of us," Raquel announced.

When everyone left for the evening, Vic gathered with Raquel, Jimmy, and Jack.

"When Lopez stated that there was no cell phone on the victim, it jogged my memory of a case we had back in the four-one. It was a drug dealer who was murdered on 138th Street. Remember the case, Jimmy? We traced the victim's cell calls and came up with the perp."

"Yeah, I do remember it. We worked the case together."

"Right! You and Jack do some research on the cell phones of the victims. See what shakes out. Try not to say too much to Fumar and his staff unless you need to. I don't know how far the corruption in this shit-hole goes," Vic ordered.

# CHAPTER 12

Raquel gave Vic the slight, side head nod to follow her into the kitchen. Vic followed behind her, watching her shapely butt and legs.

"Honey, I hope I didn't embarrass you at the end of the meeting," Raquel whispered.

"Embarrass me? You called me fat?"

"No, silly. When you ended the meeting and I went into the burlap thing. I didn't want to come across…"

Vic cut her short. "I loved it! We have to get these men thinking about putting one foot in front of another. They are smart people in a lazy, laid-back culture, I'm sorry to say."

"That's why I wanted to start tomorrow morning at seven-thirty. This ten, eleven o'clock start is such bullshit," Raquel hissed.

"When we leave, they are all going to need a two-week vacation to get back to Dominican time," Vic laughed.

"Listen, I want to spend some time with Gabby and my mom and then get into the reports, especially the autopsies. I have a feeling they've overlooked plenty."

"I'll meet with Jimmy and Jack to review some of the reports. No worries."

"And one more thing. I want to meet with some Venezuelan chicas."

"I didn't know you were swinging that way," Vic whispered into Raquel's ear, pulling her into him from her waist.

"Okay, I should have said 'interview' instead. I want to see what information we can glean from the street. Girl talk, you know. I want them to feel safe and secure and come here tomorrow sometime. I'll offer to pay for their time if need be."

"Absolutely, but I don't think paying them will be necessary. These girls are probably scared shitless and will welcome our help. Play it by ear. Okay, I'm off to the three spots."

Vic smooched his gal and was out the door in a flash with Fumar and the entourage.

In the few minutes that Vic was talking privately to Raquel, Mateo Castillo took an opportunity to break the ice with Theresa Panny. He could think of no better way than to use Gabriella as a conduit. On a table in front of a sprawling set of glass doors which led to the pool, Gabriella was working on her Mandala coloring pages. Miss Panny had printed off the "Island Vacation" symbol on Mandala, getting the site online from Google. Gabriella was using her fine point magic markers to color in the sheet of paper. Both Gabriella and Miss Panny had just sprayed bug repellant on their arms and legs. The mosquitos are brutal at night in the Dominican. Gabby and her tutor wore flowery cover ups over their bathing suits to help against the bug biting.

"That's real nice. You color inside the lines very well," Mateo blurted. He tried to sound as sincere as possible, stepping out of his Dominican cop role.

"Thank you," Gabriella uttered. The child barely looked up at Mateo. She was basically shy and untrusting of strangers, something she partly learned from her parents and partly imposed on her in her DNA.

"She really does great work, doesn't she?" Miss Panny offered.

"Absolutely. Where do you get all the color ideas, young lady?" Mateo asked Gabriella.

"My brain." Gabriella kept working, never looking up from her page.

"Which is your favorite color?"

"Blue, like this," The child showed Mateo the marker.

"Hey, mine, too. I wish my uniform was blue instead of this drab grey color."

"I like the uniforms. They look nice," Gabriella offered, this time more than just a one or two-word answer.

Theresa Panny smiled at Mateo, giving him the thumbs up sign for his rapid progress with Gabriella.

"Well, nice chatting with you. I need to go with your dad now. Have fun," Mateo said. He smiled at Theresa. Theresa smiled back and gave a cutie good-bye wave with her hand.

As tough as it was on the introverted Mateo, he was proud of himself for letting Miss Panny know he was alive.

# CHAPTER 13

"We have to do something to protect ourselves. First of all, everyone… we all must be smarter. This butcher of Punta Cana is real, make no mistake about that, ladies," Silvia announced.

Twelve chicas held an impromptu meeting on the beach in Bavaro, right near where they had all rented apartments. They were all roommates in various locations in Bavaro. Many of the chicas knew each other in Venezuela. Silvia, the oldest at thirty-two, became the spokeswoman.

Silvia continued as the girls lathered themselves in sunscreen and tanning oils.

"Since what happened to Lilly with that animal Lenny, and then Lucy with that pervert dentist, let alone all the other bullshit creeps that come along, we are all targets for violence."

"Let's not forget the two murdered in Punta Cana so far," another girl added.

"And what happened in San Pedro de Macoris. Keila was a good person, a friend of mine from back home. That motherfucker took her head off.

"Her poor family!" another blurted.

"So, what do we do? The police are useless. I know a girl who went to the cops and three of those fuckers raped her," someone called out.

Silvia held up her hand. "If we get a pimp, they take almost half, maybe more, of what we get. Then we have to blow them or whatever they want. And they are handsy, too. The best thing for us to do is work together. Watch out for each other. If groups of guys hire us, at least we are all at the same place and we can protect one another. Working alone, even walking alone, is unsafe in this country."

"The buddy system," one of the girls shouted.

"Call it whatever you want. We are here to make money and send as much as we can back home, and get back to Venezuela in one piece, and not in a coffin. Look, we are in a country where even the chicas here want to stab us. We are taking rice from their tables and they are fighting for their own survival, like we are. We must be smarter or end up in some hole in the ground."

"What about the regulars that we can trust?"

"Trust? How many of you have been smacked around by your regular clients? I have been a few times, and I know a girl who was stabbed in her belly because her regular didn't want to use a condom anymore. We all know these horror stories," Silvia explained.

"Look it…I will not screw without a condom for anyone. I can't afford some disease that will kill me slowly. I'd rather go back home and starve like everybody else in Venezuela," one girl stated.

"And what happens when we have to get our braces serviced?" someone asked.

"Get another dentist other than Fishman or go into the room together. Insist on it!" Silvia shouted.

"I heard that the police have called in some Americans to help find the killer in Punta Cana. Maybe they can help us?"

Silvia lost her cool. "Americans help only themselves. They are not going to help shit. Only we can help ourselves. Listen to me…if you want to be stupid, just know that you will be a victim. If a guy wants to pull your hair to hear you scream that's bad enough. If a guy wants to take you for a ride somewhere, you will be seeing Jesus."

"Jesus abandoned me a long time ago. I stopped believing in that shit when I was sixteen," one of the girls said.

No one spoke after that.

# CHAPTER 14

The next morning at the White House, everyone was on time as Raquel requested. Louisa made scrambled eggs with scallions and red and green peppers, crisp bacon, white toast, and a platter of bananas and mangoes. A pitcher of fresh orange juice and a large pot of coffee was placed on the table.

Gabriella, Olga, and Miss Panny had not come down for breakfast that early.

Fumar came in smelling of his first cigar of the day. His eyes were puffy like a man who drank a lot or slept little.

"Gentlemen, if you will allow me to break down some things that I discovered in your reporting," Raquel began the meeting while everyone ate breakfast. She stood by an empty whiteboard.

"Firstly, has anyone thought about the burlap that was found on each body?" Raquel queried.

Lieutenant Castillo raised his hand as if he was a schoolboy. Raquel nodded in his direction.

"I came up with a few uses for burlap. One is for landscapers and perhaps tree companies. Burlap is usually around the ball of new trees before they are planted into the ground. Also, many butchers here use burlap to move meat that has been cut up. Sometimes the meat is delivered to stores that way. Also, fishmongers are known to use burlap," Castillo stated.

"And products such as beans and coffee are transported in large burlap bags. You can actually buy small burlap bags of coffee at the airport, at the duty-free shops, and in some stores, too," Sergeant Lopez chimed in.

Vic caught a few vibes coming from Castillo and Lopez. He sensed there was a competitive barrier between them.

Raquel made a list of the burlap uses on the board.

"We can add to this list as we go forward. This is evidence that is key to the investigation, I believe. Let's keep this in mind, everyone."

Raquel continued, "I saw some things in the autopsy reports that have commonality. Each body had remnants of a common grass on them. I will need further analysis as to what kind of grass it is. I know from my research that the common grass here is called Bermuda grass. It's everywhere. I am thinking golf courses, parks, private homes and so on, so it's pretty broad.

Also, evident in each of the three victims' stomach contents was beer, dark rum in two of the three, and undigested coconut in all of their stomachs. Trace amounts of the sedative chloral hydrate was present in all the bodies. This is a non-barbiturate sedative that is commonly known in the States as a date-rape drug."

Vic chimed in, "What about the breast and vaginal wounds? Can you tell if they were similar? Were they from a right-handed or left-handed person?"

"Good question. I don't know the answer. We will have to interview the coroner to get some feedback on that. Jack, after we break, please see the coroner is notified that he is needed here soon. Later today would be great. Get one of the interpreters to get on the phone with him or her, please," Raquel ordered.

Jack Nagle made a note to himself.

Fumar jumped into the conversation. "I am shocked that these things were not brought to me before today. I'm sorry that we may have missed these obvious common elements." Fumar stared at his aides, making them all feel uncomfortable.

"Not at all, General. We have an expression in English: 'A person is too close to the forest to see the trees.' I'm sure there is one like that in Spanish. Basically, your country has not had experience with a serial killer. Our friend in the FBI headquarters in Quantico, Virginia told both of us when we worked on a major serial case that in the United States, that on any given date, there are at least six serial killers in action," Vic stated.

Lieutenant Castillo raised his hand again.

"Lieutenant, please just speak up when you need to add something," Raquel noted.

"Thank you, ma'am. I heard Sergeant Lopez mention the possibility of a watch being missing from the victim in his case. I don't recall the other two victims having anything taken from their person, unless we overlooked something again."

"Good point. Typically, a serial killer will take some item, a lock of hair, jewelry, a body part, from the victim as a memento, or souvenir, if you will. We have to dig a bit deeper into the other two homicides to see if something was missing. Perhaps the girls' friends or families can help with this information. An educated guess with this case would be jewelry, unless the girl just didn't wear her watch the day she was murdered."

"That would be an assumption, Ms. Ruiz. I was taught not to assume too many things," Sergeant Lopez blurted. Fumar cleared his throat and glared at Lopez, thinking his remark was rude.

"Excellent thought, Sergeant. Let me explain further. When we unravel a serial killer's profile, many norms have to be put aside. Not ignored, mind you, but suppositions need to be utilized. The serial murderer is vastly different than your average everyday killer. A serial killer generally plots out his victim, he studies them. That's not to say a serial can't act spontaneously. He very often has a deeply-rooted psychological reason for what he does. The victims generally, but not always, resemble one another in some way. That's why we've been asking for photos and descriptions of the murdered women. In this case, the girls have many similarities."

Lieutenant Castillo jumped in, "They all were short, brown hair and eyes, and they all wore braces on their teeth."

"Bravo," Raquel nearly hollered. She jotted down the items on the board that Castillo noted. The younger Castillo puffed out his chest with a deep inhale.

"They all had silicone-enhanced breasts as well," Lopez added.

"Another bravo," Raquel stated. She put that on the board.

Vic knew what Raquel was doing. She was getting them to think and to work as a unit.

Fumar saw this also. He was gaining confidence in his men for the first time.

The group worked together, not taking a break until eleven o'clock that morning. Fumar had chomped two cigars into mulch in that time. He nearly ran to the tiki hut to flare up a smoke. Vic pointed to Fumar's bolt to the outdoors and Jimmy, Jack, and he cracked up with laughter.

Theresa Panny and Gabriella took their breakfast upstairs, where school was in session. Olga was in the kitchen chatting with Louisa and trading their specialty recipes and stories about when they were young.

"C'mon, Gabriella, let's take a swimming lesson and have a snack. You did great today. I'm so proud of you."

"I dreamed that I swam underwater for the first time, Miss Panny."

"You're not ready for that just yet, but in time, when you are a stronger swimmer, okay?"

Theresa and Gabriella made their way to the pool. Lieutenant Castillo was waiting for this opportunity. He went back to the war room, opened his attaché, taking something from it.

Just before the teacher and her student entered the pool, Castillo sauntered over to them.

"Good morning. Such a beautiful day for a swim," Castillo declared.

"Good morning. It certainly is," Theresa responded. Gabriella was intent on getting into the pool and ignored him totally.

"Miss Gabriella, I brought you a gift."

At the word gift, Castillo had the seven-year-old's rapt attention.

Castillo handed something to the girl. It was wrapped in white tissue paper.

"Thank you," Gabriella whispered. She peeled away the paper, not letting it fall onto the ground or into the water.

It was a straw doll in a typical Dominican multi-colored floral dress. The doll was tanned, nearly brown.

"She's beautiful!" Gabriella declared. Miss Panny was beaming.

"That doll has been in my family for many, many years. It was made by my grandmother. She gave it to me to give to a daughter. I don't have a daughter, and I thought you would like it."

"I love it!" Gabriella exclaimed. The normally stranger-averse child went to Castillo for a hug. The doll was magic.

"Lieutenant there is someone at the door to see you," one of the interpreters interrupted.

Castillo excused himself from Gabriella and Miss Panny. He offered a polite wink to the teacher.

Less than a minute later, Castillo interrupted Fumar's smoke and a conversation he was having on his cell phone.

"Yes, what is it, Lieutenant?"

"Sir…there has been another homicide.

"The Butcher of Punta Cana just made himself more famous," Fumar mumbled.

# CHAPTER 15

Fumar and his men jumped into their police cars to rush to the Punta Cana Resort beach, where a body had been found. Raquel, Vic, Jimmy, and Jack got into a four-passenger golf cart that belonged to the White House. Vic and company rapidly drove through some woods, then followed a cart path adjacent to the beach toward the site. They arrived within ten minutes, getting there just as Fumar and his men arrived.

Inside a twelve-passenger boat beached in the sand was a young woman, covered in beach towels with a small burlap bag that covered her head.

Fumar barked out orders to the policemen on the scene and his men. "Everyone stay away from the boat until the coroner arrives. I want any evidence to be secured. Castillo, cordon off those tracks with the yellow tape. I want photos and molds taken of all the tracks. Do it before any wind covers them with sand! Find out who found the body and bring them to me at once."

"Looks like our guy again?" Vic asked Fumar.

"I took a quick look into the boat. It's a woman, but I want the coroner to uncover the body to see if she was cut up like the others. The burlap is visible, so I would say it's the same assailant at this point."

"It's not a Saturday, so that breaks a pattern of Friday night killings," Raquel added.

"We want to keep this murder as quiet as possible. This will be another nail in the coffin for tourism in Punta Cana," Fumar said.

Two uniformed cops brought two well-built, dark-skinned young men to Fumar. They were the ones who found the body.

"Tell me, when did you see this?" Fumar asked.

One of the men, visibly shaken, spoke nervously to the general.

"We were about to bring the boat into the water. It was about eight o'clock this morning. A group from the hotel were to be brought out to the catamaran for a tour around the area. The body was in the boat."

"Did you go into the boat and touch the deceased at all?"

"No, sir. That's bad juju. We just ran to the security guard who called the hotel. Then the police came."

"Did either of you see anyone leave the area?"

"No, sir," both men answered together.

"Okay, thank you. Just wait here a moment. Lopez, get their names and information. They are to be detained for now," Fumar ordered.

Fumar pulled Vic and Raquel to the side, close to the water's edge.

"I will try my best to do this by the book. We have learned, especially since you both got here, to tighten things up at a crime scene. I will wait here for the coroner and forensics to oversee their work. We must put an end to these murders soon, because I can tell you one thing…my job depends on finding this killer. The minister will replace me with one of his own people if we don't find this freak soon."

"I think we have enough information to build the profile. Enough of that. We will find this killer. I promise you that, Fumar," Vic blurted.

Vic and Raquel left Jimmy and Jack at the scene to be their eyes and ears and returned on the golf cart back to the villa. It was late afternoon, and the Dominican sun was still scorching everything on the ground. The New York City winter was long, cold, and wet, and Raquel loved the heat on her face.

When they returned to the White House, Louisa had prepared a wonderful fruit salad and a refreshing pineapple, mango, and guava juice drink. Batista had climbed up into a coconut tree in the front yard and cut up some of the fruit with a machete. Raquel thought of the coconut in the victim's stomach and wondered about the significance.

Gabriella was reading with Theresa under the shade of a palm tree near the pool. Olga was helping her new friend Louisa fold some laundry. Mama will never be able to get used to domestic help, Raquel thought and chuckled to herself.

Raquel had an urge to grab Vic and pull him into their bedroom for a little afternoon delight. She then thought of how inappropriate that would be, with the fourth serial murder in the vicinity in just a month.

"Honey, how about a quick dip in the pool before everyone gets back here? I really need to get some exercise and unwind," Vic called out.

"Race you to the room!"

In a few minutes, the couple were in the almost-too-warm pool water, Vic in his old man, boxer bathing suit and Raquel in her flesh-colored bikini. It looked as if she were skinny dipping. Having Gabriella did not affect her gorgeous, trim body.

The couple took a few laps together and stopped for a breather, standing at chest level in at the pool's edge. Louisa brought them a tray of her juice drink and their sunglasses to fight the glare which came off the water, nearly blinding them.

"I feel guilty doing this right now," Raquel mumbled.

"Me, too. I really wanted to grab you up in the bedroom, but that would have made me feel really guilty," Vic replied.

"I thought the same thing! Okay, after ten tonight, there can be no guilty feelings," Raquel quipped.

The couple clicked their glasses to seal the promise.

"I really want to find this fucker. I've come to like Fumar, and I'm feeling really sorry for him," Raquel stated.

"I want this killer, so we make another great payday and save a few lives. Don't worry about Fumar. Guys like him always bounce back. Anyway, I doubt he will be replaced. He's playing a head game with us a little. Typical Dominican dude."

"Excuse me, pardon me lady and sir," an older worker said in Spanish. He was in the garden pulling weeds and raking when the couple first arrived at the pool. He was closer to the pool now, having worked his way about sixty feet or so from the golf course fairway which abutted the property. Two uniformed police had been patrolling the property on security detail. They were both standing under a large willow tree near the golf course drinking bottles of water.

"Can we help you, sir?" Raquel asked in Spanish.

The worker, dressed in cream color gardening pants, a long-sleeved tattered work shirt, and a straw hat that looked like it was off the set of The Treasures of the Sierra Madre, shaded his eyes against the sun.

"I was wondering if you knew you had grubs and a groundhog in your backyard," the old man stated.

"Thank you, sir. I will tell the owner of the house," Raquel replied.

"What? What's he saying?" Vic asked.

"There are bugs and some kind of animal under the ground back there."

The man interrupted again and he began walking closer to the pool. "Excuse me, again, madam, but do you know the roses on the left side of the house need to be pruned? I never saw so much sloppy work in my life."

"Okay, sir. Please go and trim them. I'm sure you can do a better job than the last person. Have a good day," Raquel offered.

"Okay, missus. I will get to it after I call my wife. She stayed back in Lugano, Switzerland while I came here to work for you," the old guy mumbled. He began to walk back toward the back of the property, toward the golf course.

"What the hell is he saying now?" Vic asked. Vic removed his sunglasses to get a better look at the guy as he slowly walked under the shade trees.

It took Raquel a good ten seconds or so to realize what the old man said.

"Vic...what the fuck! He just said Lugano, Switzerland! That old guy is John Deegan!"

# CHAPTER 16

"So, are you proud of yourself, Deegan? You got past two cigarette-smoking Dominican policemen with that outfit you're wearing," Vic asked. Raquel and he sat across from Deegan on deck chairs under the cool shade of the veranda. Raquel used a large towel to cover up. Vic chose to drip dry.

"I fooled the two of you, didn't I?" Deegan laughed.

"What the hell has compelled you to come here? It's not as if you were invited," Raquel blurted.

"I was saying to Gjuliana the other day. I'm bored to shit. There is just so much of retirement that a guy like me can take. My cancer is gone, thanks to those great German doctors, Interpol has given up trying to find me, you guys are doing fabulously, and your daughter is a rich young lady thanks to Uncle John over here."

"There is no sense arguing with you over this. We know better than to try. Don't forget, we both chased you down from the Bronx, all over Europe, then to the Vatican, so we know what kind of a stubborn, calculating, and cunning brain you have," Raquel offered.

"And I made you both rich and famous," Deegan chuckled.

"That you did, Deegan…that you sure did," Vic stated.

"And now I'm here to help you get richer and more famous.

"It's okay, John…we got this," Raquel said.

"Well…with all due respect…I think you need to stop what you're doing and just find the killer."

"What do you mean, stop what we're doing?" Vic queried.

"Take it from a guy who went around whacking bad guys. I guess that qualified me as a serial killer. I had my reasons, and you were after me. You chased me down until I let you find me."

"That's bullshit, Deegan, and you know it. You really think you let us find you?" Vic boomed.

“Think what you want, but just because you were in the right city at the right time doesn't mean you were about to catch me. It's the same thing here. The killer will allow you to catch him. But, my old pursuers, you have to start to look for the killer. This profiling you've spent so much time on is all well and good, but now you're getting paralysis by analysis. Who cares what classification of a serial killer he is? Visionary, comfort, thrill, lust. Did you track me down based on those categories? Fuck no! Go back to what you know best…detective work!”

“How do you know so much about what we're doing?” Raquel asked.

Deegan went into his broken Spanish accent…“Lookit, mommie…a bline man can see it. Ju got all dis stuff in de hose…all fancy chit.” He reverted to Deegan, “Just get out there and knock on doors, touch the flesh. That's where the answers are. In the meantime, I have more to say. Actually, three things.” Deegan got up from the chair and brushed off his tattered work clothes.

“Make sure you put plenty of SPF 80 on Gabriella; that sun is treacherous. And keep my cell number handy. I have a sense you will need me before long.”

Deegan headed back toward the golf course in the direction of the two chatting policemen.

“Hold it a second, Deegan. You said three things. I heard only two,” Vic stated. Deegan never lost a step. He just spoke over his shoulder.

“Very good, Gonnella. I was just seeing if you were paying attention or if you have office brain. Okay, number three is obvious. That pretty young tutor you have for Gabriella. Two of the national policemen have eyes for her. Just keep an eye on that. Could be a distraction.”

While Fumar and his staff did their detailed investigation on the fourth murdered Venezuelan woman, Raquel called Jimmy Martin at the site for help.

"Jimmy, I need for you to go into Bavaro this afternoon. Bring an interpreter with you. I need to interview some Ven hookers. I want to hear what they have to say."

"How many and what time?"

"Six or eight girls. How about like seven-thirty, eight o'clock. This way we see them after we eat. Arrange for a van or taxis to pick them up. I'll ask Louisa to make some sandwiches and snacks for them. Juice, soda, no alcohol. Tell them who we are. Tell them we are trying to help them and we can pay them one hundred American dollars each for their time, okay?"

"On it. I'll call you when it's all arranged," Jimmy said before signing off.

# CHAPTER 17

"He's right, Vic. Deegan is always right, that's why he's a genius and why we are compelled to listen," Raquel uttered.

"Genius, my ass. He's just good at predicting shit."

"Okay, stay in denial. I'm going to get some of the Venezuelan chicas here tonight like I planned. I want to hear what's being said on the street. Our investigation starts tonight with getting some possible suspects. Deegan said press the flesh. He's right!"

"Let me ask you something. How does he know about Theresa? What police is he talking about? How the fuck is he here watching us all day?" Vic was stumped.

"He's probably disguised as a tree or bush or maybe he's living next door. But I can tell you one thing. A blind man can see that Lopez and Castillo have eyes for Theresa. Castillo is a gentleman and Lopez is the lady killer, pardon my pun. Let's see if the fair maiden gives her hand to one," Raquel laughed.

# CHAPTER 18

The Venezuelan girls were coming to the White House at eight o'clock that evening. Jimmy booked eight, he could have had forty. Not because it was a slow night for prostitutes, but because they were all willing to tell their story and make a quick hundred bucks without performing.

Jimmy hired a driver in Bavaro to meet the girls and bring them to the well-guarded White House in Tortuga Bay. The driver was paid one hundred American dollars to pick up and return the girls, an amount the driver could make if he hustled for two days.

At eight-fifteen, the doorbell chimed and the girls were let in by the two policemen who were guarding the front of the villa.

Raquel, Vic, Jack, and Jimmy waited under the veranda at a long table surrounded by plastic mesh chairs in front of the pool. A tray of ham sandwiches and soft drinks awaited the chicas.

'Holas' were passed all around as the normal informal greeting.

"Ladies, I am Raquel. I speak Spanish and will interpret your words to the men sitting here with us. This is Vic, Jack, and Jimmy. I think you all met Jimmy already."

The girls all stated their names. Silvia, the leader of the girls who met at Bavaro Beach, Iris, Valentina, Patrizia, Lilly, Lucy, Marianne, and Migleidy. None of the girls smiled. They were here on serious business. All of them had taken a plate and a sandwich. It was a sea of tight jeans, high heels, silver and gold bracelets, and pushed up cleavage.

"You all know why you are with us tonight. In the last month, four girls from your country have been murdered here in Punta Cana. We are private investigators here from New York to help the police find who has been doing this. We believe it was one man. We would like to hear what you have to say about the situation," Raquel announced.

Silvia was the first to speak up. "We are all very afraid. Most of us here knew at least one of the girls who was killed. Myself and Lilly knew Kleida who was killed last year in San Pedro de Macoris.

"Kleida was killed by an American man who was apprehended. He is in prison," Raquel interrupted.

"Yes, we know. Whoever this guy is in Punta Cana, he must be stopped. Most of the girls know to work together, but some continue to work alone. This is very stupid and very dangerous," Silvia professed.

"Can you express to us some things that happened to you girls and help us to look at especially violent men?" Vic asked. Raquel interpreted.

"I can. Look at my face. Look at my teeth. I don't think I will ever get my beauty back. He ruined me," Lilly cried as she spoke. Raquel gave her some tissues and patted her head. After a few minutes, she calmed down and continued her story.

"This Dominican guy beat me and raped me. He dragged me by my hair and did this to my face."

"Was he a client?" Raquel queried. She used "client" for lack of a better word.

"No, he wasn't. I will say the truth. He set us up with clients of his, and we robbed them. He came to my apartment…I was alone. This crazy man took back his client's money and jewelry we had stolen. I thought he was going to kill me, for sure," Lilly expressed.

"Do you know his name, Lilly?" Vic asked.

"He is called Lenny." Jack and Jimmy took notes on their legal pads.

"Did you report him to the local police?" Vic asked.

Silvia chimed in, "The police are all corrupt. One of my friends reported an assault and was raped by three cops. All they expect is money and free sex from us. We don't report shit after that. For all we know, this Lenny pays the police. Police…they are all pure shit."

The four Americans glanced at one another.

"Is that normally done? What I mean is, do men like Lenny often set up your clients?" Vic queried.

Valentina spoke up. She was shaking, her voice quivering. "Yes. Often. Men like Lenny, some of the caddies at the golf clubs, some taxi drivers, the house managers. They bring us to the houses and hotels where the men stay. All except the big hotel, the resort. They don't allow chicas."

"What do they take from you?" Raquel asked Valentina.

"Usually we get one hundred American dollars for two or three hours. The clients pay the men who bring us. We usually have no idea what the johns are charged. Could be one fifty, or two hundred. Sometimes we get tips for extra work."

"Explain the extra work, please," Raquel asked. Valentina was embarrassed and put her eyes down.

Silvia picked up the question. "In the ass. A blow job with no condom. Some men want to be hit with a stick or a belt. We charge extra in the room for any of that."

"Tell us some more close calls, ladies," Raquel queried.

"One girl was burned by a cigar… all over her back while the client held her down. When she went to the hospital, one of the men who worked there attacked her," Silvia added.

"A sensitive question. How many clients do you usually see in a day?" Jack asked. His light Irish skin reddened at his bold question.

"It depends on the day," Marianne blurted. "Sometimes two. On a Friday night, it's much busier, and sometimes three men will be serviced."

"Why is Friday busy?" Jack followed.

"Many of the tourists arrive on Fridays, so there is more demand. Saturdays, too. But Sunday is quiet because the men leave or are drunk from the weekend," Silvia answered.

"Any other dangerous or creepy men can you tell us about?" Vic asked.

"There is a dentist…I hate this man. Many girls go to him to get their braces adjusted. I know he does nasty things. I went to him to take out two teeth. He put me under with gas and other shit. I think he did things to me and another girl while I was there. He is a seedy, ugly, smelly man," Lucy said.

"Did he rape you, Lucy?" Raquel asked.

"I would have to say no. My jeans are too tight to get off easily."

All of the girls laughed at the way Lucy stood up and shook her booty. The Americans cracked up as well.

"What is this dentist's name?" Vic asked.

A few of the girls answered in unison. “Fishman!” Duly noted by Jack and Jimmy. Jimmy looked his name up online on his laptop. Joel Fishman had an office address in Punta Cana.

Just then, Theresa, Olga, and Gabriella came outside to say good night.

“Ay, how beautiful she is,” Silvia exclaimed. A few girls agreed with Silvia.

Partrizia and Migleidy dabbed tears from their eyes, thinking about their own small daughters back in Venezuela.

“Thank you. She is a mini-me,” Raquel added.

Olga looked at the girls, not remarking, but her eyes told a story. She was old school and did not appreciate women making money in the oldest profession. Olga thought there were many other ways to make a living.

Gabriella smiled and went right to her mom for a goodnight hug and kiss. She jumped onto her dad’s lap for a long hug and kiss.

“Daddy’s girl!” one of the chicas blurted.

Theresa said her good nights and took Gabriella upstairs to read her a good night story. Olga headed into the kitchen to eavesdrop.

The group loosened up and started talking about home and their parents and children, how difficult life was now in Venezuela, and how wonderful it was when they were little girls, when there were good jobs and plenty of money. The chicas remained for another hour, telling stories of johns who just like to hit them, and also how many men were kind and generous to them.

The Americans understood the desperation in these women’s lives and why they turned to prostitution. The story was a sad one, with survival on everyone’s minds.

Before they left, Vic asked one parting question.

“Among the regular clients you all have, who is the most generous and the most regular?

Silvia led the answer with all of the girls murmuring and agreeing.

“The Cuban guy we call the coffee king. That man loves chicas. Two at a time usually.”

"The coffee king. I see. Where does this Cuban live?" Vic asked.

Silvia answered emphatically. "He has the biggest house in all of Punta Cana. At Punta Espada."

"Is there anyone else you think could have murdered these poor girls?" Jimmy blurted.

"That handsome guy at Punta Espada. And he owns a company that services the gardens and grass at the villas. He tried to choke me one time with a plastic bag over my face. He said it was a game. I still have nightmares from that time," Valentina stated.

"At the golf course?" Vic asked. The suffocation attempt peaked the four American's interest.

"Yes. There are a few golf courses. I think he is in charge of a couple of them."

"Valentina, do you know this man's name?"

"I don't remember it."

"I do," Iris answered. She put her head into her hands and began to sob.

After she composed herself, Iris spoke in a near whisper.

"His name is Fernando Reyes. He goes by Freddy. I am so afraid of that man. I've been with him more than a few times. At first, he seemed normal and sweet. And yes, he is very handsome. Truthfully, I started to fall for him. Like I wanted to be his girlfriend. He led me to believe he and I…" Iris began crying again.

"Take your time, sweetheart," Raquel whispered, putting her arms around the shaking girl.

"Anyway, he turned violent one night. I didn't want to tell anyone because I was afraid he would come after me, or that I would get sent back to Venezuela. He has a lot of politician friends who play golf at Punta Espada."

"You said violent. What did he actually do to you?"

"One night, very late, he sent for me to come to Punta Espada. No one was there. Freddy wanted to have sex with me on the golf course overlooking the sea. He said it would be very romantic. I believed him. I was falling in love, I think. He took me on a big golf cart. It was so dark, I couldn't see my own hand in front of me, and I was afraid. We had sex in the golf cart and he was hurting me, so when I pushed him away, he dragged me by my arms to the rocks by the water." Iris paused. She looked out into the night with a heart-wrenching stare as if she was reliving the trauma.

"It's okay, Iris. Can you say what he did to you?" Raquel asked gently.

"I'll try. He threw me onto the rocks. Some of the rocks were coral and they cut my feet. I could hear the sea smashing into the rocks. I was naked, and the water was trying to pull me in. He said, I will kill you here, throw your body into the water and that nobody would ever find me. I begged for my life. He lit a cigar, then he threw my clothes onto the grass and drove away. I walked for so long until I finally found a path, and then finally some lights that led me to some homes. An old woman helped me. She called for a taxi for me."

The entire group went silent, feeling the horror that Iris went through.

"I never told anyone what he did to me that night. Not until just now. I never saw him again, and I hope to Jesus I never will."

# CHAPTER 19

"Fumar, gentlemen, last evening, we met with several Venezuelan girls to whom we reached out in order to gather some intelligence. Our discussion garnered a few leads that we think should be looked into immediately," Vic announced. The meeting started promptly at seven-thirty with Louisa's breakfast offering of pancakes, sausages, and eggs.

"How would you like us to proceed?" Fumar questioned.

"Well, I can tell you how I don't want to proceed. No local police can either be used to bring the suspects in, nor should they be aware of anything we are doing. As a matter of fact, I want all of the local police off our security detail," Vic hissed.

"No issue at all. I can bring in national police if you wish, but may I ask why?"

"The girls told us a few horror stories. I must tell you all that I believe every word they said. The local cops are corrupt, they take advantage of these women up to, and including, rape. Now we all know the reputation of the police in this country, so let's not kid each other. Fumar, I mean no disrespect to you and your men here with us. Let's just say we don't want any leaks or warnings sent out from this house."

"Vic, I take no insult from your words. Lieutenant Castillo will call La Capital and we will be fully manned with three shifts, all hand-picked men by this afternoon," Fumar spouted. Castillo excused himself from the table.

Raquel piped in, "There are four suspects we want to look at. I'm not putting their names on the board for the reasons Vic just outlined, so please take your own notes. There is a dentist in Punta Cana. Doctor Joel Fishman. I want to begin by going to this man for a consultation. I will be wired. Jimmy and Jack will be with me, right outside. The girls reported that he did certain things that were inappropriate. Look, he may just be your everyday, run-of-the-mill creep, but let's see what we come out with. The girls seem to all know him, and all have had unique and disturbing visits with Fishman. Second, we want a street guy "Lenny" brought in for questioning and to face assault charges today. Jack got a written statement from one of the girls that implicates him in a violent encounter, including rape. And there is a third name that requires some additional information and research."

"May I ask about the other two suspects?" Fumar asked.

"Of course. The girls call one of them the Cuban coffee king. Evidently, he has a big house on the Punta Espada golf course. Anyone heard of him?" Vic offered.

"His name is Ralph Ledon. One of the richest men in the Dominican Republic. He has Cuban and Dominican citizenship, and he is close friends to the Castros and to Danilo Medina, our president," Sergeant Lopez preached.

"How do you know this?" Fumar questioned his man.

"He is also a close friend of my father. I've been to his house several times. He runs benefits for various charities. His parties are amazing. The Clintons, Manny Sousa, Baryshnikov, Julio Iglesias, like that."

"What kind of a man is he?" Raquel asked.

"What do you mean? Like…?"

"Family man? Player?"

"Absolutely both. I think he has children about my age from a first wife. His new wife is much younger, from a Cuban family that was close to Fulgencio Battista before he was deposed. Her family emigrated to Miami back then."

"Okay, let's keep that information within the confines of this group, please. This sounds a bit sensitive, so we need to tread lightly. Let's discuss an approach to Mr. Ledon after we look at the other three…agreed?" Vic stated. No one dissented.

Raquel chimed in, "We have to do some research, but the fourth evidently works at Punta Espada golf club. A few things that were said about him are indicators. His name is Fernando Reyes."

"Freddy? That's crazy, I know him, too," Lopez blurted.

"I hope he's not a good friend of yours, Sergeant," Raquel said icily. Fumar glared at the sergeant.

"No, not a friend at all. He gets a few of us passes to play the course. I mean…he's a great guy…at least…"

“That’s enough, Sergeant. You are ordered to stay away from him and to not to mention this to anyone. Understood?” Fumar yelled.

“Yes, sir.”

The group of investigators and police began making their plans to look into Lenny, Doctor Fishman, and Freddy.

Raquel was about to call Fishman’s office for an appointment when Gabriella came bounding down the marble staircase toward her mom. Theresa was a few steps behind.

“Good morning, my love!” Raquel bellowed. Gabriella jumped up into her mother’s arms.

“You are getting so big, Gabby. Pretty soon I will be jumping into your arms!”

“Mommy, can we go to the beach today?”

“If all of your lessons are caught up, I don’t see a reason why not.”

“Okay, abuelita said she would come, too, but she has to bring an umbrella because of the sun.”

“Daddy will make sure there are plenty of chairs and umbrellas and water and juice, and Louisa will make some sandwiches and snacks.”

“Mommy, I have a question. Miss Panny never answered my question. Those ladies that were here last night. Why were they here?”

Raquel paused, looked at Theresa as if to say, ‘now what?’

“Well, honey…there has been some trouble here with women from another country. I told you back home that mommy and daddy had to come here to help fix the problem, remember?”

“Yes, I remember. What do those ladies do for work? Are they actresses or models?”

"Let's say they are for now, my love. Actresses and models. That's close enough. They are always acting and showing off their beautiful clothes… so, let's get you started packing for the beach…what do you say?"

"Okay, mommy, but those ladies are all so pretty and dressed up. I want to be just like them when I grow up," Gabriella spouted.

Olga, who just came into the room, caught what her granddaughter said.

"Maybe God will take me tonight in my sleep!" the abuelita spouted as she blessed herself three times and spit into her open collar.

# CHAPTER 20

Raquel was able to get a three o'clock appointment with Doctor Joel Fishman. The receptionist claimed there was a cancellation that afternoon and that the doctor would be there. The group prepared their plan and headed at 2:30 to the strip mall not far from the White House.

Wearing tight jeans and an off-the-shoulder blouse, Raquel placed a tiny recording device under the lower band of her bra, using adhesive tape to hold it in place. Jack was outside in the parking lot in the Cadillac Escalade, Jimmy was stationed outside in the hallway waiting to pounce if necessary. Four of Fumar's national police were in the parking lot in two unmarked sedans awaiting instructions from Jack.

Raquel filled out the required paperwork for a new patient and sat in the waiting room thumbing through a Spanish People Magazine.

"What a pretty woman," Fishman began in Spanish. Raquel was brought to a dental chair by the receptionist who only worked until three.

"Why thank you, doctor," Raquel replied in English.

"Perfect! I don't get a chance to speak my native tongue very often here. Where are you from, Ms. Ruiz?"

"I'm a New York City girl."

"I'm from Brooklyn, originally. All settled here in Punta Cana now.

"The Dominican Republic is very beautiful."

"What brings you here?"

"Do you mean Punta Cana or to this office?" Raquel played coy.

"Both."

"I'm thinking about relocating here. Getting a condo, maybe open a nice boutique."

"That's exciting, I'm sure I can refer some of my patients to you. I take care of many young women. Ninety percent of my practice. Lots of braces," Fishman smiled.

"Yeah, almost every young woman I see down here is wearing braces. What's that all about?"

"In the DR, they have no insurance and no government assistance. Somehow, these girls find the money. It's all cash for me. Now, the girls from Venezuela, who are all over the place these days, had their braces put on for next to nothing back home. Then they come here to work the tourist trade. The thing with braces is that they have to be maintained on a weekly basis. That's where I come in."

"The tourist trade?" Raquel asked, feigning naiveté.

"Yes, they're hookers. Venezuela is starving. The girls are very attractive and make lots of cash and send it home. After they pay me, of course," Fishman laughed.

"Interesting."

"So, what brings you here, Ms. Ruiz? Is it Ms. or Mrs.?"

"Ms. I just finalized a divorce."

"He must be an insane man to let you get away."

"That's sweet."

"Anyway, do you have a dental issue?"

"Not really, I'm here because I need a local dentist. I need a cleaning. Maybe x-rays. You know, a checkup."

"Let's take a look." Fishman lowered the overhead lamp, shining it into Raquel's eyes. He took a dental probe and a mouth mirror. "Open," he instructed.

As Fishman stood over his patient, Raquel got a whiff of his sour breath. Her stomach turned a bit and she held her breath. The dentist put his hand on Raquel's bare shoulder and rubbed himself against her arm. She could feel his erect penis through his pants.

"You've really taken care of your teeth. You have a gorgeous smile, Raquel. May I call you Raquel?

"Of course."

"I'd like to take some x-rays and maybe an impression or two. I see a slight mal-occlusion in your bite."

"What does that mean?"

"Your bite is not perfect. Your uppers and lowers are a tiny bit off."

"What needs to be done?"

"We have a few options. Let's start off with an x-ray. Would you like some sweet air to calm your nerves?"

"I'm really not nervous. What's sweet air anyway?"

"Some air that will take the edge off. Like a drink or two. It's relaxing."

"Why not?"

Fishman set up the nitrous oxide mask, putting it over Raquel's mouth and nose.

"Breathe deeply, Raquel. Just go with it."

Raquel held her breath and pretended to be groggy and out of it. Fishman did what Fishman does. He immediately put his hand down his patient's blouse, fondling her right breast.

"What the fuck!" Raquel screamed.

In a flash, Jimmy Martin was in the operatory, grabbing the unsuspecting degenerate dentist by his arm, pulling it around his back and nearly breaking Fishman's wrist. The dentist screamed out like a little girl.

"You piece of shit!" Raquel yelled.

Jack and Fumar's four men crashed into the office.

"What's going on here?" Fishman hollered.

"Toss the fucking place. Look for any sedatives, anything that this creep can use to paralyze his patients. Look for any knives, too," Jimmy ordered.

"What is this? I want to see my lawyer!"

"Fuck you and your fucking lawyer. What do you think this is, the United States? I'll read your Miranda rights? I'll bash your head in for you, motherfucker!" Jimmy exploded.

Fishman was cuffed and brought into his waiting room. A young Dominican patient walked in for the dentist's next appointment.

"Sorry, the dentist is closed. Go home!" one of the policemen ordered.

Jack, Raquel, and three of the policemen rummaged through the drug cabinet and the drawers in the operatory. They ransacked the desk in Fishman's office; any cabinet or drawer that was in the place was tossed. After several minutes of searching, Jack came up with something interesting in the drug cabinet. He examined every single drug or liquid in the box until he found what he was looking for.

"Bingo!" Jack yelled.

"What is it?" Raquel asked. She was still just a bit shaken by the experience.

"Chloral hydrate," Jack announced.

# CHAPTER 21

"Our suspect known as 'Lenny' is one Lenin Diaz. He's a Dominican citizen, born in Boca Chica in '86. Lenny was a hustler back home, mostly in the flesh trade, some cocaine dealing, but no arrests. Anything goes in Boca Chica; it's a wide-open town, and Lenny had a lot of police friends, it seems. The inspector of police is a friend of mine and a straight shooter. He called Lenny a cockroach. Diaz has two kids there that he doesn't support. Unfortunately, this is very common in the Dominican. Lenny came here to Punta Cana ten years ago. Looks like he has a few key friends on the police force here. Very generous with money," Sergeant Lopez stated. He was speaking to Vic, Fumar, and three of his plainclothes men.

The general's eyes narrowed, making them look like those of a serpent. "Where can we find this Lenny?" Fumar asked.

"He works mostly around the airport and out of a local bar, Mi Casa Lounge. He gets the girls mostly for Americans and Canadians, as his English is understandable. He also hustles underage girls, mostly for the German male tourists," Lopez replied.

"Perfect. I'll be his next client," Vic announced.

Vic's cell phone chimed. It was Raquel.

"Hi, we collared this creepy fuck," Raquel declared.

"Did he follow his M.O.?"

"He sure did. Tried to put me under and grabbed my tit. Jimmy nearly pulled his arm out of its socket and smacked him around a bit."

"Sorry. Any other evidence?" Vic queried.

"Oh yeah. He had a few vials of chloral hydrate."

"NO SHIT?" Vic exploded.

"Yup. We're taking him to the warehouse at Naves Bavaro for a detailed interrogation. These people don't play."

"I love this country. Interrogation the old-fashioned way."

"Shall we wait for you?" Raquel asked.

"Yeah, keep him on ice. He may have a roommate soon, if things go as planned. I'll be in touch."

Vic walked into Mi Casa Lounge dressed in shorts, a Callaway golf shirt, flip flops, and a Yankee baseball cap. Vic had that New York swagger that said he was someone not to fuck with. Two of Fumar's plainclothes men were already at the bar, while Fumar waited in an unmarked car with two other national police.

"Hola…how are ju, el guapo?" Vic was greeted by a tall, Dominican blonde in a green evening gown, with her breasts, screaming to be let loose, and a split up her dress that rose to her thong.

"Hola, what is the bartender's name, mi amor?"

"Who needs hin? I will take care of ju personally. My name is Stella."

"Maybe I'll come by later. What's his name, Stella?"

"I call him dick face. His name is Pepe."

Vic ambled to the bar, sat down, surveyed the bar as if he owned it, and ordered a Jameson, neat.

"Thank you, Pepe."

"Ju know my nane? Ju been here before, my frien?"

"You forgot me? Victor from New York...two years ago."

"Ju do look familiar. All ju Italian guys fron New Jork look and soun like Robert DiNero or Al Pacino, all the sane."

"You like the movies?"

"All of then. Godfather, Casino, Scarface. Except Pacino don sound like no Cuban I ever knew."

Vic laughed. "I agree. Listen, Pepe. I got eight guys here from New York. We're playing golf and need some entertainment. My friends are heavy hitters. Someone gave me Lenny's name. Do you happen to have his number?"

"Of course. We work together, my frien. Lenny should be here berry soon, but I can call him for ju and get hin here right now, no proglen."

Vic passed a twenty over the bar for Pepe.

"Gracias, my frien. I call now," Pepe said.

Pepe moved to the end of the bar, fast punching numbers into his phone. He spoke softly and hit the red button.

"Fibe…maybe ten-minute Lenny be here, Bictor," Pepe whispered.

Twenty minutes later, Lenny walked into the lounge. Pepe made the introductions. Victor was now his "ole frien from New Jork."

Lenny invited Vic to a table off the bar. The bar was dark and smelled of beer, piss, and cheap perfume. There were several chicas sitting with doofus-looking guys in golf attire at the bar and the tables.

"Pepe said ju habe eight guys here? In a villa?"

"Yes, in Tortuga Bay. Nice place. Can you provide entertainment?"

"Das what I do, my frien. All quality chicas. But is sontines hard to get chicas past the guards at Tortuga."

"I'm sure you can figure that out, Lenny."

"Okay, an maybe a nice tip to Lenny?"

"Sure. Do you have photos of these ladies? My guys are very, shall we say…demanding. They don't want to spend their money on pigs."

Lenny took his phone and put it on the table.

"No pigs fron me. For three hundred American dollars, I can show ju the finest Benezuelan chicas ju will eber see in jour life."

"Let's take a look. If they are first class, that's no problem."

Lenny opened his phone, pressed his photo icon, and gave the phone to Vic.

"Ju scroll to the leff."

Vic looked at the girls. He recognized a few of them.

"Wow, I want this one!" Vic exclaimed. He pointed to the phone.

"No proglen, my frien. What tine ju want them?"

"How about eight-o'clock tonight. For three hundred, they spend the night, right?"

"Oh no, my frien. If ju want dem to stay, ju pay more to dem."

"No way! A few years ago, I paid a hundred."

"No now my frien. Deez are Benezuelans. Much better chicas. Much better looking, and dey do whatever ju want to dem, beliebe me. An, listen to me, none over twenty-three."

Vic took his Yankee cap from his head. A prearranged signal for the police to move in. Fumar and his men left the car and made their way into the lounge. The two cops at the bar moved slowly toward the table where Vic and Lenny sat.

"So is that what happened to Lilly Bianchi, Lenny? She let you do whatever you wanted to her, you rat fuck," Vic stood from his chair. Lenny stood up as well.

"What the... I don know no Lilly..."

The two undercover men grabbed Lenny and pushed him back down into his chair. "Keep your hands on the table, 'my friend' if you don't mind," Vic snorted.

Fumar walked slowly to the table so everyone in the place could see him coming in his decorated uniform. Some of the girls ran out a door at the back of the bar.

"Mr. Lenin Diaz. I am arresting you for the assault and rape of a citizen of the Republica Bolivariana de Venezuela, who is here on a temporary visa, Miss Lilly Bianchi. Other charges may be brought against you. Frisk him and take him," Fumar commanded.

# CHAPTER 22

"Doctor Fishman, I am not a violent man. That is to say, I'm not prone to violence. However, my career in the national police means a lot to me and to my family. It's a matter of pride for my parents and grandparents that I rise up through the ranks. I'm sure you know what pride is, doctor. Your parents must have been proud of you when you became a dentist. Isn't that so?" Lieutenant Castillo asked.

"Naturally, they were. 'My son, the dentist!'" Joel Fishman replied.

The slightly-built dentist was sitting in a beat-up, dark wooden chair, the kind you see behind the desk of a school teacher. Fishman's arms were latched to the chair's armrests, his small hands swelling from the pressure of the tight tape that bound him.

"So, now that we understand one another a little, I am going to ask you a series of questions. I expect complete honesty from you. If I feel you are not telling me the truth...well. Let me say you will see a side of me that you can't even imagine by simply looking at me."

Castillo was standing ten feet from Fishman's chair, which was in the middle of a large, empty warehouse. This was a modern facility, with rows of metal shelving on one side, and room for dozens of wood pallets on the other. The Dominican government was using the place for "storage."

There was no single bulb over the dentist as you would see in a movie scene. There was plenty of light still coming through a skylight. Sundown wasn't for another thirty minutes, but when it did finally get dark, overhead LED lighting would flood the room.

"Sergeant, please see to it that your men bring some bottles of water and a few towels. We may be here for a while," Castillo uttered.

"Yes, Lieutenant," Lopez replied. Raquel, Jimmy, and Jack sat in metal folding chairs to the left of Doctor Fishman, within the shaking dentist's field of vision.

"Okay then. That officer sitting over there with the laptop will be taking notes of our conversation. At the end of this session, a document for your signature will be submitted to you. So, let's begin, shall we?"

Fishman looked as if he were going to pass out. His thin, fake dark hair was matted to his head, as he was sweating profusely. His beady eyes were darting all over the room, and the stink of his breath and flatulence permeated the area around him.

"Doctor Fishman, tell me what you do on a typical weekend. More specifically, what do you do on a Friday night?" Castillo asked. The lieutenant paced five feet in front of the chair to which Fishman was bound.

"I'm sorry, what is this all about? What did I do that was so wrong?"

"Please, doctor, just answer my questions."

"Well, geez, let's see. Well...I sometimes go to have a few drinks. Sometimes I drive to La Romana, I don't know. Different things."

"How about last Friday evening. Where were you, doctor?"

"I'm so nervous I can barely remember. Let me think a second. Oh God! I was at Onno's Bar in Bavaro. That's right, I went to Captain Cook for dinner and then to Onno's."

"Captain Cook? On the beach?"

"Yes, that's the place."

"About what time did you get to...

"Six thirty, I leave the office early on Fridays. Then I go out for a while."

"Alone?"

"Yes, I'm alone."

"No steady girl?"

"No...no."

"Chicas?"

Fishman was visibly uncomfortable with the question. He glanced over at Raquel.

"Come now, doctor, we are all adults here. Do you frequent the chicas?"

"Yes."

"What kind of chicas do you prefer?"

"What do you mean? Skinny ones. I like skinny."

"I was referring to nationality, Doctor Fishman." Castillo got close to the dentist for the first time.

"Truthfully, I like them all."

"Do you prefer Dominican chicas or Venezuelan chicas, doctor?"

"Look, if this is about those murdered girls, I can assure you, I had nothing at all to do with that."

"We shall see, now, won't we?"

"Dominicans, doctor. Do you prefer Dominican ladies?"

"I prefer the Vens. But I didn't hurt anyone, God as my witness."

"Hurt is a broad term, now isn't it, doctor? You can hurt someone in many ways. We have reports that you have molested a number of your female patients. You also molested that woman sitting over there. How do we know how far you are willing to go?"

"Okay, yes, I have done some of those things to my patients. It's unethical and wrong. I have a problem. I've done it before. That's why I had to leave the States. I'm sorry."

"We know why you left the United States, doctor. Now let's get back to some questions. The night you went to Onno's bar, were you with a chica?"

"No."

"No? Really, doctor.? And why is that, and why do you recall that you were not with a woman so quickly?"

"It's difficult for me to say that in front of the woman."

"I was a New York City cop. I've heard it all, Fishman," Raquel blurted.

"Well, I had just satisfied myself with one of my patients…okay?"

"So, you are admitting to sodomy and rape, Doctor Fishman. We certainly will check out what you have told us so far, but we will have many other questions. You will remain in custody while we continue our investigation. Let me ask you one more important question that I have on my mind," Castillo offered.

"I did not kill anyone…I swear!"

"We found some very incriminating evidence in your office, doctor. Why do you have chloral hydrate? Is that to knock out your patients so you can abuse them sexually?"

"Absolutely not!" Fishman hollered.

"Then, why have it?"

"Very simple explanation. I have pediatric patients. Some as young as two or three years old. I administer an oral regimen of hydrazine and chloral hydrate. This sedative has been widely used and deemed safe and effective for treating young and uncooperative pediatric dental patients. I can show you the records of the patients I have used it on. I'm a very good dentist, sir."

"Not any more, doctor. You've treated your last patient in the Dominican Republic," Castillo added.

# CHAPTER 23

"Mr. Diaz, 'Lenny,' my man, I'm sure you can imagine what will happen to you if you do not cooperate with me tonight. I am a man with very little patience for bullshit. My men with me? They are professionals; they are trained to get confessions out of criminals such as yourself. I suggest you answer my questions truthfully and completely. For your own benefit," Fumar commanded.

Lenny, like Fishman, was tied to a chair with heavy tape in a similar warehouse room in another part of the building. Two of Fumar's men, beefy policemen who were well experienced with interrogation, sat on either side of the suspect in metal folding chairs. Vic sat to the side, glaring at Lenny to aid in the intimidation factor. Another man sat at a table made up of boxes with a laptop to record the event.

"In your own words, please tell us what your profession is, Mr. Diaz," Fumar asked.

"My profession? I really don't have a profession, sir."

Fumar looked at his man who sat to Lenny's right. The burly cop, wearing black leather gloves, rose from his chair and smacked Lenny hard across his face.

"Don't be coy with me. What's wrong with you? I just told you I lack patience."

"I do things for tourists. I arrange many things for them. I've been here for ten years without one single arrest."

"Not true. You are arrested now, Mr. Diaz. You will have a hard time in our prison system, I assure you. So now, tell me what exactly do you arrange for tourists?"

"I stay mostly at the airport. Because I can speak English, I get transportation for people, I set up fishing trips, boat trips, and sightseeing tours, set up golf times...you know...things like that."

Fumar glanced at the policemen at Lenny's left. The cop nonchalantly stood from his chair and punched Lenny hard in his solar plexus, doubling the hapless and hopeless man into a ball. Lenny began coughing and sucking for air, his eyes bulging, his bald head shining from sweat.

"Now, what else do you do, Mr. Diaz? Stop the bullshit. These men will pummel you all night. They actually enjoy this part of their jobs."

Lenny struggled to speak.

"I…I get the tourists chicas. And sometimes drugs."

"That's better, Mr. Diaz. I'm curious, what kind of drugs?"

"Marijuana and coke. That's all." Lenny flinched, thinking his answer was not what the general wanted to hear.

"What kind of chicas, Mr. Diaz?"

"Sir, please I don't understand the question. What kind?"

"Yes. Ages, nationality, race?"

"Oh, I see. Right now they are mostly Venezuelan. Before, Dominican and Haitian. Depends if the men like whiter or blacker."

"And how old are these girls?"

"Nineteen or twenty to about thirty or so."

"Any younger? Mind your answer, Mr. Diaz," Fumar warned.

"Yes, sometimes very young. Twelve, thirteen. These girls are mostly for the Europeans. Mostly Germans, some Americans."

"You are aware that pimping is illegal in this country, and the penalty can be ten to fifteen years in prison?"

"My God, you don't have enough prisons to put all the people who get women to have sex for money. Every bartender, caddie, cab driver, hotel clerk, and cigar guy has a list of girls. Why single me out? What I do is good for the economy. These girls can at least feed their children."

"That is a matter for the judges to decide. The law is the law."

"That's a lot of bullshit, and you know it!" Lenny exploded.

Fumar smiled broadly at the police enforcer on Lenny's right. This time he smashed Lenny across his face with a closed fist. The force nearly toppled the chair onto the warehouse floor. Lenny almost blacked out from the punch. A line of blood oozed from his nose.

"Now then, Mr. Diaz, I have some more questions. I advise you to step down from your pulpit and answer truthfully."

"What are those cuts and scrapes on your hands, Mr. Diaz?"

"Someone robbed clients of mine, and I took care of the problem. I regret it, but I admit it."

"So, you are saying those bruises came from the brutal beating you gave Ms. Lilly Bianchi in her apartment in Bavaro?"

"Yes, sir."

"And you anally raped her and urinated on her?"

"I did that. Yes."

"Ms. Bianchi said that you got back the money and items that she and her friends stole from your clients. Is that true, Mr. Diaz?"

"I got back most of what was stolen. Yes."

"And you returned it all to your clients?"

"No, sir, I returned a small amount. I kept most of what was stolen," Lenny admitted. He was afraid to lie, not knowing if the police knew the answer to the question.

Fumar stood from his chair and got up into Lenny's face. The general's voice was just above a whisper. "I think you are lying about getting these wounds on your hands from beating that poor girl. Do you want to know what I think, Diaz? I believe you scraped your hands on the coral when you placed that murdered girl in the cave at Punta Espada. I believe you have violently killed four women in Punta Cana. Four that we know of."

"I swear on everything I love, I never killed anyone. I beat that puta, yes, I did. But I never killed anyone. Never!" Lenny looked his accuser dead straight in his eyes.

"So, who did kill those girls, Mr. Lenin Diaz? You are now an admitted pimp, rapist, and drug dealer. Who would you think we should be putting in the chair you are now sitting in?"

"I know some things, some things that may help you find who you are looking for. If I help you, can you..."

"If you help us, the only thing that will stick to you is public urination," Fumar stated.

"Okay, there are people you should be looking at. For instance, there is the couple that have real estate right nearby this house. They rent out villas and they are into some really kinky shit. No one would ever believe what I know. They are both very good looking. From Europe someplace, I don't remember, maybe Denmark or Sweden. The wife is a gorgeous blonde, and the husband is a tennis teacher. They have a couple of kids. Looks like the perfect happy family. I banged the wife myself while the husband took a video, but they are mainly into S&M shit. I provided chicas for them, and the girls had to get extra money for the shit the people wanted them to do," Lenny submitted.

"Vic, this man wants us to believe that just because a couple has a different sex life, they have murdered four women in the past month. I hope he has more to offer us, otherwise he will make a good girlfriend for someone in our prison. I think for him, La Victoria prison is the right place for Lenny to meet his mate," Fumar offered sarcastically.

"Sir, there are others. Maybe my best client is the killer. He has a huge appetite for Venezuelan chicas. Only Venezuelan, and the best of them. I gave him many girls. He keeps their pictures and phone numbers in his phone. He paid me well, so I don't care that he goes directly to the girls. Sometimes the girls are roughed up by him, but they enjoy the big money. But no one will believe he is like this because he is a big-shot."

"Tell me his name," Fumar demanded.

Lenny swallowed hard. He paused a bit too long for Fumar's liking.

"Diaz, do you need a bit of a memory enhancer?"

Lenny blinked hard twice and uttered the name. "Ralph Ledon."

Vic caught Fumar's eyes for a scant second.

Fumar put his face two inches in front of Lenny's face. Fumar took a freshly lit Churchill cigar from his mouth and blew on the lit end.

"You know what I'm told? I'm told that this cigar is about five hundred degrees when I don't puff on it. But…when I do take a big puff, it can be as high as eight or nine hundred degrees. So, my friend, Mr. Diaz, stop fucking with me, or I will take a giant puff and place this motherfucker right on your pretty little nose."

Lenny felt the heat from the cigar near his face and tried to pull his head away. The two bully cops held hapless Lenny's head steady.

"Sir, I swear. This is what I know. I know I didn't do these things. All I am telling you is about some people who are weird. Maybe it's not them, but at least I'm trying to tell you all that I know," Lenny begged.

"Okay, Diaz. I will knock on the front door of Mr. Ledon, one of the richest men in the country, and ask him if he murdered some chicas. My boss will get a call from Medina, and I will be working at the airport, flipping burgers. Don't play with me, Diaz, you pimp." Fumar inhaled his cigar deeply and puffed the smoke into Lenny's face. The general looked at the burning cigar tip and smiled.

Vic interrupted the drama. "General, I believe we should now let Mr. Diaz think about his options for a while. Lock him up here overnight. We will resume questioning tomorrow. But this time, I will insist that you get the answers we are looking for out of him."

Fumar gave Lenny a look of disappointment. "These Americans have laws that protect scumbags like you. They are soft, but because he is my guest, we will start all over with you tomorrow. I will not be so nice, Diaz," Fumar spouted. Lenny smelled the cigar on his captor's sour breath and gagged.

"You will be gagging a lot in La Victoria, my friend," Fumar quipped.

# CHAPTER 24

Fumar kept Doctor Fishman and Lenny Diaz on ice for a few days while the investigation continued. Vic played good cop with Lenny, bringing him food and toiletries and things, all the time chatting him up. Jack did the same with Fishman, who was crying like a child the whole time, professing his innocence and sobbing about his mommy issues.

Sergeant Lopez, invited by his father, asked Vic and Raquel to attend a black-tie charity gala at the Punta Espada clubhouse, an event that could not be missed on a number of levels.

"Honey, you are turning heads in this place. How does it feel being the best-looking woman at the party?" Vic gushed.

"Flattery will get you lucky. Stop the bullshit, though. Have you looked at some of the women here tonight? I'm starting to feel my age. It looks like the Playboy mansion, for Christ's sake," Raquel responded.

"That's my story and I'm sticking with it."

That morning, Raquel had shopped in the fancy stores at the Punta Cana marina while Vic strolled along looking at the magnificent yachts lined up at the docks like they were postage stamps. He picked out his outfit for the event, a classic black, single-breasted, conservative tuxedo.

"I absolutely love what you picked out, Raquel. Stunning!" Vic commented.

"You ain't so bad yourself, Mr. James Bond. Just keep yourself at my elbow. Puerto Rican women are known to stab."

The grand ballroom at Punta Espada was lavishly decorated for Christmas in March by a foundation started five years ago for the benefit of an orphanage in Santo Domingo. The foundation was chaired by its founder, and former orphan himself, Ralph Ledon.

Nearly five hundred guests attended the formal event, with the fanciest and wealthiest people in the Caribbean in attendance. Air-cooled tents were placed outside the ballroom's exterior doors, which faces the eighteenth green. The green itself, and part of the sea next to it, was lit for dramatic effect in the colors of the Dominican flag: white, red, and blue.

Thirty tuxedoed, white-gloved waiters passed silver trays of mini Cuban sandwiches, sushi, lamb chops, and a host of other hors d'oeuvres.

"Who would have thought the Dominicans would outdo my people when it comes to prosciutto? This is the best I've ever had by far!" Vic mentioned.

Raquel was busy looking around at the flowers, the luminaries, and the gorgeous dresses worn by the lady guests...and even one or two who didn't really look like ladies.

Vic continued his review, "I've never really seen it carved off the full leg before. And it tastes incredible."

"What's that, honey?"

"The prosciutto!"

"Really, Vic? That's what you're fixated on? I barely got into this dress, and you're pushing the prosciutto. I'll eat when we get back to the house," Raquel blurted.

"But just look at this freakin' place. The food looks amazing, the music is fabulous, people can smoke, I even saw a few ladies with cigars," Vic said.

Raquel leaned in and whispered, "Yeah, all you noticed was their cigars, you dog. Remember, we are here for a reason."

"Geez, of course."

A waiter presented a tray to the couple. "Peking Duck?" The dark, crispy duck slices were atop a wafer-thin Chinese pancake with cucumber and spring onion slices.

Vic grabbed hold of one, dipping the tasty duck into a side dish of hoisin sauce and popping it into his mouth. Raquel politely demurred.

"Are you certain, Miss? They are delightful," the waiter asked.

"I'm sure, thank you."

The gown Raquel wore was an amazing dark green, off the shoulder number that had a snake-like texture to its fabric. The dress formed around each curve and bump on Raquel's toned body. Her brown hair cascaded down her back, just above the off-the-shoulder collar. Raquel's elegant neck and natural olive skin tone was perfect without any jewelry around it. A slit from the bottom of the garment to Raquel's mid-thigh gave her shapely legs the glimpse every man in the place was hoping for.

"That is an Oscar de la Renta! I wish my dear friend Oscar was here to see you in his creation. Simply stunning!" none other than Ralph Ledon declared as he and his wife passed by.

"Yes, it is de la Renta. Thank you," Raquel replied.

"Please allow me to introduce myself. I'm Ralph Ledon. This is my wife, Lissandra Hoyos-Ledon, it's my pleasure, I'm sure."

"Mr. Ledon, I'm Vic Gonnella, and this is Raquel Ruiz, my partner."

Lissandra was a stunner. Considerably younger than her husband, she looked more Castilian than Cuban. Large, deep, dark eyes, almost jet-black straight hair that fell to the top of her perfectly-formed butt, lips that were perfectly puffy and pouty, and a body that would make most men kill a blood relative to be with. Lissandra, like her husband, were the only people in the room who wore white. She, in a white silk formal pantsuit, with a diamond and ruby choker that needed its own zip code. Ralph wore a white tuxedo with a black shirt and white tie.

"I am so happy to meet you both and to welcome you to my adopted country," Ledon replied.

"This is a marvelous gala, Mr. Ledon," Raquel stated.

"Please, I am Ralph. Mr. Ledon was my father, and he was killed, along with my mother, by the beard in Havana when I was in the cradle. I prefer informality."

"So, I suppose that is why you have founded this wonderful charity?" Vic queried.

"Yes, indeed. I was born into a well-to-do family in Cuba. Coffee people, ironically. Castro took everything, including my parents. I was in an orphanage in Cuba for a year or so, and then a Dominican family paid to get me out of there. I'm sixty-three years old this year...well I think I'm sixty-three, they never had an original birth certificate on me, but the Dominican Republic has my heart. And you? Where do you call home?"

"I'm a Bronx girl, Puerto Rican parents. We live in Manhattan now."

"Ahh, the great land of the valiant and noble lord," Ralph uttered.

"Pardon?"

"That is the meaning of the word Borinquen."

"Really, I don't think I ever knew that," Raquel replied.

"Well, now you do!" Ralph laughed. "And you, Victor, where do you hail from?"

"I'm a Bronx boy. Family is from Sicily and Italy. I did that blood thing last year and it said I was seven percent European Jew. That was surprising."

Lissandra joined into the conversation. "I have Jewish blood as well. Sephardic Jews were all over Spain, where almost all of my ancestors are from. They settled in Cuba long ago."

"Were you born in Cuba?" Raquel asked.

"Yes, I was. Until this wonderful man stole me away."

"Well it was indeed as if I stole you, wasn't it? You see, I was in Cuba on business, and I saw Lissandra working in a hotel at the front desk. One look, and I was struck by lightning. I am fortunate to have a few contacts in high places in Cuba. A month later, Lissandra was with me. Soon after, we married."

"Any children?" Vic blurted.

"No, no children," Lissandra replied. Her answer was uttered in such a way as though there was a regret, or an underlying reason why there were no kids. Vic and Raquel felt an uneasiness among the Ledons.

*Me and my big mouth!* Vic thought.

Ralph broke the awkward moment, "Well, it was a pleasure to meet both of you. Enjoy the evening. Thank you for attending tonight. We must make the rounds, of course."

Raquel and Vic smiled and raised their glasses to the couple as they made their exit. They both followed Lissandra with their eyes, albeit Vic's eyes were lower.

Putting her hand under Vic's arm, Raquel steered them toward the outside tent to where the music was coming from.

"Honey, that was not a good question. She seemed very sensitive about not having kids," Raquel whispered.

"I know. I should have kept the topic on heritage or something else. I blew it!"

"Yeah, just a little."

"He's a dynamic guy, don't you think?" Vic asked.

"Since when is creepy a synonym for dynamic? The guy was undressing me with his eyes the whole time. Didn't you see him looking at me and licking his lips like fucking Hannibal Lecter? And… with a wife who looks like that, he must be fucked up totally. Why is he using prostitutes, Vic? What the hell is wrong with men, anyway?"

"A friend of mine always says, now it's a friend of mine…not me…my friend says, 'behind every gorgeous woman is a guy who's sick of fucking her.'"

"That's gross. That's sick. Just tell me when you get sick of me, will ya?"

"Jesus, I said my friend said it, not me. It's a theory some…"

"Quit while you're ahead, Gonnella."

"Wow, look at this place. I would love to play golf here before we leave," Vic mused.

"We're not doing so good on this case, Vic. We need to hit the pedal and solve this bitch," Raquel whispered.

"Speaking of...did she seem bitchy to you?" Vic asked.

"Who?"

"Lissandra. Did she seem bitchy, in a way?"

"Not at all. But there is just something about her that made me sad. Maybe it's the no children thing or the older husband thing or the fact that I know he is a creep. Listen to me, honey, if I knew he was a creep in five minutes, she certainly does."

"I think we keep Ralphy high on our suspects list," Vic offered.

"Oh, yeah!"

# CHAPTER 25

"Well, Mr. Diaz, you, had a few days to think about things. I bet you haven't had too much sleep. Here we are again. I don't think I have to remind you of my temperament," Fumar stated.

"No sir, I remember what happens when you are annoyed," Lenny responded.

"What else do you have to say about the murdered girls?"

"I didn't murder anyone. I have been violent at times, but never…"

"Shut the fuck up! You almost killed that girl. You beat her senseless. You likely damaged her face for life, to say nothing about pimping her, raping her, and pissing on her. You have a very brutal personality. I have a question, Diaz. At what point in your life did you think you were this tough guy?"

"I… regret my actions, but I assure you, I am not a tough guy, and I am not this butcher you are seeking."

"The only thing you regret is getting caught and facing a long prison sentence. After awhile, you will get used to taking it up the ass and sucking dicks. How many girls were violated by you that we don't know about? My offer still stands. Help us to find the killer and you walk."

"I never did that type of violence to a woman before. Yes, I lost my mind that night. Yes, I had smacked a few chicas around, but my word to God, never like that." Lenny's lips quivered as he stifled a sob.

"Tell us more about why you think one of the pillars of the community, Mr. Ralph Ledon, had anything to do with the murder of these four women?" Vic queried.

"Because some of the girls told me how he hurt them. He paid double, sometimes triple, to keep Venezuelan chicas coming back to him. And he made his wife participate."

"Participate?" Vic added.

"His wife, and she is a real beautiful woman, would be ordered to watch him with the chicas. Only Venezuelans. Sometimes he would make his wife join him to have sex with the girls."

"And his kinky ways makes him a murderer?" Fumar questioned.

"I can't say that for sure. But the bodies were all found not far from his villa. Just think about that for a minute. He was always particular about the look of the girls. Thin, light-skinned, big fake tits, brunette…a certain type."

"Did you send any of the murdered girls to him at any time?" Vic asked.

Lenny paused. He put his head down, and shook his head in the affirmative.

"I can't hear your answer, Diaz," Fumar shouted.

"Yes…yes I did."

"Which girl, Lenny?" Vic queried.

"Her name was Pamela. A real beauty. She was the one found at Punta Espada."

Vic looked at Fumar. He gave the general a head nod to walk away from the chair to which Lenny was tied. The two men walked to the other end of the warehouse.

"Pamela Leon. Her name was never released to the press," Vic noted.

"To me, that means nothing. I'm sure many of the Venezuelan chicas knew of her. This joker likely heard of her name. Besides, if he was the killer…he knew her name."

Vic and Fumar went back to Lenny.

Fumar took a long pull on his cigar. "Mr. Diaz, we are still going to hold you on the charges that we outlined. And, also now, we are holding you on suspicion of murder. You will be held temporarily at the prison in Higuey. In solitary, for your own protection."

"What? No! I'm innocent!"

"My God, you are ruining me. Just throw me out of your country… I am still an American citizen," Fishman cried.

"Let me see. You molest patients, that is called rape in your country... and it's called rape here as well. But in your country, you can get away with that crime so long as you have enough money and good lawyers. Now doctor, we have checked on your use of sedatives. Specifically, hydrazine, chloral hydrate, and nitrous oxide. You are absolutely correct. These chemicals are used for some pediatric patients. And further investigation shows that your records are complete, as you stated. That still does not mean you never used the sedative chloral hydrate on unsuspecting prostitutes," Lieutenant Castillo stated.

"Look, I have a sickness. I will be totally honest with you. I've used a drug to...to have my way with some women, but I never killed anyone. I am a repeated sex offender at most, not a killer."

"What drug or drugs do you admit using on these girls, doctor?"

"Ketamine. That's all. Never chloral hydrate...never."

"Maybe you are saying this because you know we found chloral hydrate in the system of the murdered girls," Castillo offered.

Raquel spoke up, "Ketamine...Special K. How do you get that, doctor?"

"I have a source. I'd rather not say."

"Doctor Fishman, remember when I said I am not a violent man? Well, I'm not a pushover, either. Answer the question, or these men with me will be asked to fuck you up," Castillo hissed.

Fishman began to sob again.

"Who is your source, doctor?" Castillo shouted.

"Okay...okay, all I know is his first name...Lenny."

# CHAPTER 26

The night sky was filled with stars, and the fresh, salty breeze off the ocean made for a magical evening for Vic and Raquel.

"Oh, Vic, honey," Raquel sighed. "Isn't it just so beautiful here? It's just...just so sensuous!"

Vic had no idea if his lady meant the room, the house, the country... but he didn't care. They'd been working non-stop on this case, and Vic's usually strong libido was demanding attention.

"Honey," he said. "YOU are sensuous," Vic whispered as he came up behind her on the deck outside their room, wrapping his arms around her waist as he leaned in to smell her hair. She brushed her hair to one side so Vic could nuzzle into her neck and sniff her new, special perfume that she'd bought just for this trip. "Mmmmmm," he said.

Raquel turned around and smiled at her lover. "What's say you and I, um, do it out here?" she whispered as she slowly leaned in, giving him a passionate, wet kiss.

Vic, laughed and said, "and give the security guards a story for a lifetime? How about we pass on the patio and..."

With that, Raquel put her finger to Vic's lips to quiet him, then gently took his hand and led him back into their room where they found themselves entwined on the king-sized bed.

"Oh, yeah," Vic moaned when Raquel went down on him.

"Hush!"

Raquel stopped what she was doing for a second and laughed because most times during their passionate, hours-long love-making sessions, Vic had to quiet her down. As things progressed, this night would be no exception.

“Is it just me, or is our sex getting better?” Vic asked when they were catching their breath.

“I’m telling you, it’s this island. I think we should buy a place down here one day. Or at least get here on vacations. Not that you aren’t the sexiest man in the world wherever we are, but you also know what happens to me when there's a full moon! It makes me crazy. Mmmm, I’m ready to go again, baby,” Raquel purred.

Vic quietly howled and the two broke into laughter. “I need a few minutes. My equipment is designed slightly different than yours, my love. Let’s chat about the case for a bit.”

“What? That’s a mood breaker! Okay, but you're not going to get away from me and sit on your laptop or fall asleep on me, Vic. A woman has needs, ya know!"

"You're a maniac, and I love you," Vic replied.

"Okay, twenty minutes of business, then we get back down to business!" Raquel, totally nude, jumped out of bed, grabbed two waters, and plopped herself back on the bed, sitting up cross-legged.

"Deal," Vic said realizing it was going to be hard for him to concentrate. He still found her enormously attractive and sexy, more attractive, in fact than any other women he knew. *I am one lucky guy*, he thought.

“This case is no lay-up. I thought we would come here, analyze the evidence, make a few inquiries, a quick arrest, and enjoy the sun for a few days,” Raquel offered.

“The connection between Fishman and Lenny. What do you think about that angle?" Vic asked.

“I'm not sure. Punta Cana is a small, big place. Most of the locals, the full-time residents, have one or two degrees of separation. For all we know, Lenny gets his teeth fixed by Fishman,” Raquel said.

“I know! When you told me Fishman got Special K from Lenny, my whole thought process changed on the both of them. Yeah, they might not fit the classic profile of a serial but…together? Who knows?”

“Oooh! Together? I never thought about that." *He's so smart AND sexy. I really am the luckiest girl in the world*, Raquel thought. "But I’m stuck on a few things. The burlap. What is it about that burlap? Let’s get Jack to investigate that angle and see if it's all coming from the same place. And keep pushing the girls for information. I think Jimmy should get different girls this time. I'll get them here for another interview. Christ, I can't believe the situation they have to put up with back in their homeland. All those poor people. I read that the average Venezuelan has lost like twenty-six pounds in the past year."

"It's a shit hole for sure. That's socialism for ya!"

"Vic, I'm worried. What if these leads are all dead ends? I want to take a closer look at that Danish couple, too. I really think we have to expand the field, honey."

"You are so friggin' sexy. How about you make this expand," Vic said as he glanced down at himself.

"Thank God!" Raquel teased as she straddled him. "That was the longest twenty minutes of my life!"

At seven-thirty in the morning, Fumar and his men, Vic, Raquel, and their crew met for breakfast.

Olga was up early and actually helping Louisa prepare breakfast. They were having a great time starting a huge Puerto Rican-style pernil for lunch. Theresa and Gabriella were also up early on the veranda enjoying the morning sun, preparing for a swim lesson. Theresa was wearing a modest bikini this time, her hair pulled back in a tight ponytail.

Raquel started the meeting. She was full of energy. "Gentlemen, we need to redouble our efforts on a few things today. If you don't mind, I will break down some of the things Vic and I would like to get going on. Jack, please follow the burlap angle. Let's get the analysis of the burlap to see what kind of burlap it was and what, if anything, was ever inside the bags. I don't think I saw anything in the reports on that, so do your best to narrow things down. Jimmy, let's get a fresh batch of girls here today. Maybe they will offer some more leads. Try for lunch at one o'clock. They can still get to work at night. Offer the same amount, transportation too, like before.

"Also, I think the connection between Fishman and Lenny may bring something. Fumar, they are your prisoners, so perhaps you can…"

Fumar interrupted. "Yes, Raquel, I already discussed this with my men. We are going to change things a bit. I am going to interview Fishman and get tough on that runt. Lopez and Castillo will team up on Lenny. I promise it will be interesting."

"I like it. I only wish we could have done what you do when we were on the NYPD," Vic blurted. Fumar grinned through his unlit Churchill.

"This morning, I'm going to look at that Danish couple that Lenny threw under the bus. I don't think people with two kids and a great life in Punta Cana would decide to strangle and mutilate prostitutes for kicks, but it's a lead, and I want to follow it," Raquel announced.

"Lieutenant Castillo, do you have anything you would like to add?" Raquel inquired.

Castillo was a bit distracted, trying to see Theresa in her bikini at the pool. He snapped back into the meeting.

"Ah, yes. I have something I thought about last night when I was going over the map of where the four bodies were discovered. In two of the cases, we found the murdered victims were brought where they were found by some sort of small vehicle, like a golf cart, or that type vehicle. We have some molds and photos of the tire tracks. Also, in looking at the area where the bodies were found, I believe the killer is actually murdering the girls within a six or seven-kilometer radius. There are a lot of golf carts on the courses, and many villas have golf carts as well. I believe we need to canvass the area to look at as many carts or cart-like vehicles as we can."

"Lieutenant, if I may?" Sergeant Lopez interrupted. "How do we find golf carts that are closed up inside of the garages in the villas? This seems like a daunting task. You know, the needle in the haystack." There was a touch of sarcasm in Lopez's voice. Rolling his eyes showed no respect for Castillo.

"I would prefer to at least follow every possible theory than sit around and wait for yet another body," Castillo fired back.

Fumar jumped in, "I agree with Castillo. We must try. Lieutenant, pick three squads of two men each. Pick the best people we have. Explain the importance, and give them copies of the tire photographs. Make sure you are keeping accurate records of what places we are canvassing. Start immediately."

"Yes, sir." Castillo stood, saluted, and left the meeting. As he headed for the door, he turned back to look at the bikini-clad Theresa at the pool one more time.

Lopez could tell that Castillo was smitten by the American teacher. He also noticed Theresa's amazing body. He decided to put all of his Dominican charm to work as soon as the situation allowed. He knew if he got to her, Castillo would be angry.

# CHAPTER 27

The bedroom was a massive mix of marble and mahogany. Green and white speckled Italian terrazzo floor tiles, heavy ornate wood furniture with a four poster, European, king-sized bed, and recessed LED spotlighting gave the room a breathtaking look. The lights, in various hues of green, red, and blue, shone onto the bed, with a white and orange backlit wall giving the entire room an almost eerie, melodramatic look.

"Lissandra, get in here now!" Ralph Ledon screamed. The coffee king was waiting for his young wife to join him and a twenty-year-old Venezuelan stunner.

"You are a pig. I told you I didn't feel very well tonight. Go get another chica and make her your third," Lissandra shouted.

"Get in here now, you fucking bitch!"

*I hate him. I wish he dies of a heart attack tonight. I want to see him choke. I can't stand another minute of this shit,* Lissandra thought. The coffee king's beautiful young wife slowly made her way from the downstairs living room, up a grand marble staircase, and to the bedroom suite.

"I'm coming, okay? Just give me a minute."

As Lissandra approached the door to the bedroom she shared with her husband, the unmistakable stifled moans of a woman sent a chill up her spine.

"Come on, my love. I want you to lick her while I pound that culo. Lay under her," Ralph ordered. He was naked except for a bright white Panama hat he was wearing. The girl was wearing black spandex pants with the crotch area torn off.

The miserable girl, her brown hair matted and sticking to her sweat-drenched back, was on her knees, her legs and arms each tied to a pillar of the bed. In her mouth was a red breathable ball gag, which was attached around her neck by a black leather strap.

"Get down on her Lissandra and pull on my balls. Make the bitch cum!" Ralph instructed.

A few moments later, the wretched chica began to feel Lissandra's hot, moist tongue on her. Both women fake moaned to help Ralph along. The poor girl kept thinking about the money, one thousand American dollars for maybe two hours work. Lissandra wasn't thinking anything. Her actions were on autopilot.

The pounding and licking went on until Ralph's knees began to cramp.

"Okay, you slut, let's see how you moan when you are choking," Ralph announced.

Ralph was behind the young woman, intermittently penetrating her rectum and her vagina. Lissandra stopped licking for a moment, pretending to be enjoying the sadistic acts.

Ralph pulled hard on the black choker, cutting the girl's air supply. Realizing she was about to be choked to death, the chica pulled hard on her arm restraints to no avail. She could feel rapid tingling in her face, the prelude to passing out. Her bulging eyes became a faucet of tears as they started to lose light. Suddenly, Ralph released the pressure on the girl's neck, just as he came into her.

"Oh, my God, that was the best...the absolute best," Ralph gushed. "Lissandra, you made me very happy tonight. Wait until you see what I'm getting for you. You will be the happiest woman in the entire Caribbean. You will love me even more. You do love me, don't you?"

"Yes, my love. Of course I do."

The chica was trying not to sob, the red ball still in her mouth. The girl felt pressure in her bowels and the need to urinate. She couldn't hold it, shooting pee onto the satin sheets and expelling an acrid gas at the same time.

"Jesus Christ...Ralph, please release her and get her the fuck out of here, will you? And get someone to burn these sheets," Lissandra blurted.

*If he would only die, my life would be heavenly. How I hate this pig!* Lissandra thought.

# CHAPTER 28

"I have to tell you that you and Raquel both looked great. That gown she wore the other night was simply amazing. And you were not so bad yourself, a cross between Dean Martin and Sean Connery," John Deegan stated. He had called Vic on his cell.

"You saw us leaving the villa, I suppose?"

"Not at all. I was at the gala. Wonderful event."

"You were *what?*"

"I was at the gala. I actually interacted with you and Raquel," Deegan snickered.

"Stop the bullshit, will ya?"

"You gobbled that Peking Duck like you were starved."

"Areyoukiddenmeorwhat? You were that fucking waiter?"

"No, I was that fucking server. I'm a serial server," John guffawed.

"I'll be a son of a bitch! Wait till I tell her. She is going to flip out."

"Anyway, back to business. I looked out my window this afternoon and saw yet another group of beautiful Venezuelan, ah… what are they called, chicas?"

"Why do I feel like you're gloating because we haven't closed this case yet, John?" Vic replied.

"I never expected you to apprehend this killer in less than a week. As an old friend and advisor, I must tell you that the killer is right under your nose."

"I told you back in Rome, you are not an old friend. You are John Deegan, a world-wide, wanted serial killer who has a lot of money, who got away with his crimes because I was stupid and weak. As far as advisor, I will listen to the devil himself if it helps pull this guy inside."

"Bringing the girls in was a brilliant idea, but you can forget the dentist and that Lenny character. Degenerates indeed, but this is an island full of degenerates and not only the tourists. Focus on the evidence, Vic. Focus on the things right in front of you. I'm having so much fun with this, I really am," Deegan hit the red button on his cell phone.

*Typical. He throws shit out there and leaves you hanging. Asshole!* Vic thought.

# CHAPTER 29

"You are the most beautiful and talented young lady in all of the Dominican Republic," Sergeant Manuel Lopez said to Gabriella Gonnella. He had returned to the war room to gather some information that he conveniently left behind.

Gabriella and Theresa were putting the finishing touches on her Mandala coloring pages.

Gabriella looked up from the page at the handsome sergeant, offering a shy smile.

"You should say, 'thank you,' young lady," Theresa added.

Gabriella ignored her teacher's words.

"It's the age. I'm sorry," Theresa mouthed.

"May I introduce myself to you both? My name is Manny. I live in Santo Domingo, La Capital."

"I'm Theresa, I live in New York, La Apple," Theresa laughed.

"Saint Theresa, the Little Flower. My mother is devoted to that saint."

"So is mine!"

"How do you like the Dominican?" Lopez inquired.

"I haven't seen much. Just this gorgeous villa and the beach, but the little I've seen is amazing. Is the weather always perfect?"

"Perfect until it pours. Then it's not so fun. This is not the rainy season. Just a few sprinkles at night at the moment."

"I heard the rain and saw the fantastic lightning show last night."

"Theresa, I have a question. Do you get any time off from your duties?"

"Yes, I do. I was thinking about taking a catamaran tour in a few days."

"I would be honored if you would allow me to escort you around Punta Cana. Only thing is, I can only take off the day after tomorrow, this Sunday," Lopez held his breath in anticipation.

"That may work. I just have to clear it with Raquel."

Lopez handed Theresa his phone. "Okay, Theresa, the little flower, put your number in here. I'll text you, you text me. Hopefully I can pick you up around nine on Sunday morning so we can get a lot in. Sorry, but I have to get over to the prison now. Hope to see you then." Lopez said a quick goodbye to Gabriella, and off he went.

Thirty minutes later, Lopez joined Fumar at the Higuey prison.

"Doctor Fishman, I am Lieutenant General Esteban Disla Martinez of the Identification and Investigation unit of the Ministry of Interior and Police. I am in charge of the case of the four women who have been murdered in Punta Cana in the last month."

"I told the other police I had nothing to do with this. I admitted to some other things, but I'm not your man," Fishman whimpered. The dentist was tied to the chair in a stark conference room at the prison.

"We shall see. We shall see. I will tell you, I am not a patient man. Things are done differently here than in the United States. If I believe you are lying or holding back facts or evidence, it will not go well for you today."

Fishman looked tired and pale. He was held in solitary in the prison's lower level. No sunlight, only water and a bit of food was given to him.

"Tell me about your use of sedation. I'm particularly interested in your association with this Lenny, from whom you sourced Ketamine," Fumar said. He sat in a chair three feet in front of the accused. His two police goons were standing on either side of Fishman.

"I don't know too much about him. Only that he can get the drug, and other drugs too, and he offered to get some women for me," Fishman choked out his words.

"But you have your own women, isn't that right Doctor Fishman?"

"Yes…some of my patients."

"I see. So, you never used any of his stable of Venezuelans?"

"Never. Just the drug."

"And how often did you get the Special K from Lenny?"

"I don't remember. A few times maybe."

Fumar looked at the fat policeman on Fishman's right side.

The cop went behind the unfortunate prisoner. He squeezed his head tightly at both ears, then let go and smashed his beefy hands against Fishman's ears.

The dentist screamed out in pain. He began to sob. His head felt as if it were going to explode.

"'I don't remember' and 'a few times' is not an acceptable reply, doctor. Try again," Fumar yelled.

"Three times, I think. I would meet him at the bar where he was. He never came to my office. He didn't know what I was doing with the drug."

"And the chloral hydrate? Lenny provided that as well?"

"No…no. I ordered that from a medical supply company for legitimate dental application. I swear."

"You expect me to believe that you used chloral hydrate only for your pediatric patients, knowing what is does to an individual, but you only used the Ketamine for your adult female patients? Please, doctor, don't insult my intelligence," Fumar seethed.

A quick glance from Fumar, and the cop on Fishman's left stepped up in front of the unlucky dentist, tightened a black leather glove on his right hand, then buried his fist into the tied man's stomach.

Fishman doubled over in pain. His breath was gone. He began to suck in air for thirty seconds before he vomited onto his prison shirt and prison pants. His lap was covered in foul-smelling mucus.

Fishman caught his breath after a minute or so.

"I only gave those girls Ketamine. And some nitrous oxide. That's all I did…I swear it."

"How did you come to know this Lenny?" Fumar asked.

"From the lounge in Bavaro. I went a few times for drinks and to see what was going on there. He approached me. He offered me girls and cocaine. This area is full of guys like Lenny. It was my bad luck to hook up with him."

"I am going to make you a one-time offer, Doctor Fishman. Be sure you listen to me very closely. Assuming you did not kill these women, I want to know who did. You help me, and I will help you. I will see that you are immediately deported for your crimes instead of spending twenty years in this hell hole."

Fishman wailed like an injured animal. "Don't you think I would tell you? Don't you know that I will not survive in a jail here? I want to see the American Ambassador. I am still an American citizen."

Fumar leaned closer to Fishman. The acrid smell of puke and urine made the general pull his head back.

"Right now, my pathetic man, you have no country."

# CHAPTER 30

"Today may be your lucky day, Lenny. Well first off, I'm not going to beat the shit out of you, so you're ahead of the game. Second, if you help me, I'll help you. We can work together," Vic declared.

They were in the warden's office at the Higuey prison. The office looked like the warden was a partner in a New York law firm. Cherry wood walls, a four-foot-high antique oak cigar humidor, a huge, black mahogany desk with a massive, brown leather chair, full bar in the corner, plush maroon and gold fabric wing chairs, a Persian carpet… the works.

Lenny was in solitary confinement on the opposite side of the jail from where Fishman was being held. When he was walked through general population to meet with Vic, Lenny knew full well he would be a mark for the career criminals at Higuey.

"Over here, baldy. When you come into this section, you will be my fucking bitch, I promise you!" an inmate screamed.

"Yo, I got something right here for you, slick. You will swallow and like it, faggot," another yelled.

"Whatever I need to do to stay da fuck out of dis place…I'm in," Lenny declared.

"Don't blame you. First off, tell me about that dentist Fishman. That weird looking dude. He was a client of yours, I understand," Vic queried.

"Not with chicas. I dink he may be half-a-fag. I only sold chit to hin."

"Chit?"

"Yeah, you know, drugs."

"Oh, I see, shit. Which drugs?"

"I dink only special K. Das it."

"What was he using the K for?"

"What eberyone uses it for, I guess. Put it into drinks and get girls all fucked up. He can't get laid without money or drugs, dat ugly motherfucker."

"You know what I think? I think he might be the one that's killing those chicas," Vic offered.

"Dude…look at hin. He can't even…he a fucking jerkoff. I hope he did kill then so ju will leabe me be, but I don' dink so. Unless he had help, he couldn't move a body ten feet."

"That's someone's theory in the Ministry of Police in La Capital. He killed the girls and paid you big money to help stash the bodies," Vic lied.

"Dat is son fucked up bullshit, right there. No way!"

"Okay, let's forget him for a while. Tell me more about that Danish or German couple you mentioned."

"Dey tell me ju know is not me and it's not dat faggy Fishman. You're still looking for dat killer," Lenny blurted. He smiled at Vic for approval.

"You're a pretty smart guy, Lenny. Not the run-of-the-mill scumbag. Let's look at what we have here. If you cooperate with me, I put in a good word with the general, maybe he helps you out a bit. If you don't help me, I really didn't understand what those guys were saying to you on the way up here, but I think I get the idea. That can't be fun, Lenny."

"Are ju crazy? Maybe the general will help me? He hate my guts. This is no like I see on American telebision where de bad guy help dem out and dey make a legit deal. Eberyone here is a cock sucker and a liar."

"I'll get the deal done. On my word. Lenny, you've got absolutely nothing else to go on at the moment," Vic reasoned.

Lenny paused to weigh his flimsy options.

"What do ju have in mind? Ju know I have no choice."

"I know. You're a knucklehead, Lenny, but I kind of like you. I promise if you don't make me look like an asshole, I'll make good. So here is what I need from you. I get you out of here and you set up that blonde couple with a Venezuelan chica, someone they would like. You've worked with them before, so you approach them with a real beauty. Some prime chocha. We pay the girl big, and she wears a wire. We listen in, if they make a bad move, we move in. If they don't, at least the guys will have a nice time listening."

"I'm no real loved by the Benezuelan chicas, my frien. It difficult right now."

"Seeing that your asshole depends on it, you better figure it out, Lenny."

"How much pay to me?"

"Nice try, fuck head. You have balls bigger than Andrew Carnegie."

"Who?"

"Donald Trump."

"Jajajajajaj. I get it. I got bigger balls dan Trump."

# CHAPTER 31

"I'm thinking we may need to reach out for help," Vic blurted. The couple was having their morning coffee in the shade of the veranda near the pool in their white, cotton, Turkish bathrobes, on the lazy, sunny Sunday morning.

"Deegan?" Raquel asked.

"Oh, not to worry. We won't have to ask for his help. I'm expecting a visit with the name of the killer out of him any day now. He came here because he's bored to death in Switzerland. I'm just wondering how he found out we were on the job."

"Who knows what he knows and when? Scary smart, I think Deegan's been referred to as."

"I was thinking more like calling Gail Gain at Langley," Vic uttered.

"G.G.? I love her! I always thought you had a thing for her, honey," Raquel teased. She brought the coffee mug to her mouth, giving her man a sexy wink.

"Well, she does have a high pay grade and a great FBI pension."

"But Lewandowski said the FBI passed on the case, remember?"

"G.G. is brilliant. I'm not asking her in any official capacity. I'm just thinking she could review what we have so far, ya know, just the major points of the case to see if she has any suggestions."

"I'm not opposed to reaching out to her, I'm just nervous word would get out that we're stumped," Raquel worried.

"I don't think we are stumped. Not yet, anyway. It's just that things move very slowly down here. Only the killer is moving quickly. Four killings in as many weeks is not too laid back. I want to have more activity… more shit going on. We're still waiting for Lopez and the analysis on the burlap, for Christ's sake. Jack said Lopez is waiting for a report."

"Yeah, and we haven't heard squat on the canvassing on the golf carts. That's if the tire marks were even made by a golf cart. Maybe it's another type of vehicle," Raquel suggested. They both sipped some coffee. Vic took a bite of sliced mango that was on a platter Louisa had left in the fridge for them.

"I think I need to have a come to Jesus meeting with Fumar and his team," Raquel stated.

Vic ignored Raquel's comment, almost as if he was preoccupied. "It's Sunday and still a bit early in Langley. That's even if she's in on a Sunday," Vic muttered. He was staring out at the golf course like he was daydreaming.

"Vic, I have her cell and home number. Maybe you're just not really ready to call her. If you think calling her is an admission of defeat or giving up, you're way off. We need to use anything and anyone to help catch this guy," Raquel preached.

Just then, the front doorbell of the villa rang.

"Who the hell is ringing the bell this early on a Sunday morning?" Vic asked.

Batista, the house boy, was watering the plants in the indoor gardens. He moved quickly to answer the doorbell.

"Oh, It's probably Lopez. I forgot to mention it. He's here to pick up Theresa," Raquel informed.

"Pick up Theresa? For what?"

"She asked for the day so she could see Punta Cana. Lopez is off today and he's going to show her the sights."

"He's going to show her something, all right."

"Cut the crap, will ya? He's single, she's single. So what? They've both been working very hard. It's just a date, Vic."

Batista let Lopez in, giving the Sergeant the hand shake, shoulder bump routine.

"Yankees kicked ass last night," Batista whispered.

"Too early in the season," Lopez followed.

Theresa ambled down the staircase looking radiant. Batista was so dumbstruck that he almost fell into the garden he was watering.

"You look lovely," Lopez exclaimed.

“Gee, thanks. I didn’t bring many clothes. I hope this isn’t too casual?” Theresa inquired. She was all legs. Her khaki shorts were not exactly Daisy Dukes, but they weren’t Catholic school girl-style either. A pair of tan espadrilles made her long, tanned, athletic legs difficult for Lopez not to gawk. A light blue halter top just showed a peek of her flat abs, yet displayed enough of her breasts to keep them mysteriously desirable. A pair of sunglasses rode atop a blue, New York Mets baseball cap, her hair dangling in a pony-tail, giving her the look of a perky college girl, ready-for-fun look.

Lopez had to work hard to be the cool Dominican man, but he was thinking, *Holy shit!*

“You look nice yourself, Manny. I can’t wait to see Punta Cana!”

*I can’t wait to see those clothes on my hotel room floor,* Manny thought, then he rebuked himself. *This is a nice American girl, Manuel, don’t fuck this up.*

The sergeant looked very different outside of his stiff uniform. He wore slightly baggy, black, linen slacks, brown sandals, and an untucked, squared off, short-sleeved, cream colored guayabera shirt. A woven eighteen carat gold chain hung from Lopez’s neck, passing the first button on his shirt.

“Hey, guys, what a great day you’ll have! Perfect Dominican weather,” Raquel announced. She came out into the foyer to greet Lopez and kiss Theresa. Vic was having no part of it. He chose to remain under the veranda.

“Thank you, ma’am,” Lopez managed to get out. He was feeling a bit out of place, coming to call on Theresa.

“See you later, Raquel. Thanks for the day,” Theresa gushed. The tutor hugged her employer, and off she and Lopez went in his not new, army green, unmarked police car.

Raquel rejoined her man near the pool.

“What, are you crazy? I don’t like it. Not one bit. We don’t encourage this kind of thing in the office, so why accept it here?” Vic demanded.

“It’s not the same.”

"How is it not the same? We are here to do a job. To catch a killer, and our daughter's tutor is out with one of the investigators. And by the way, did you see how she looked?"

"Oh, so, you peeked from your hiding spot? So, tell me, Vic, how did she look?"

"I wasn't hiding. Just…awkward, I thought. And she looked very good. I mean, she's a pretty girl."

"Typical. I swear you would drag yourself over broken glass to see a nice ass. Men are such pigs!" Raquel exclaimed.

Vic made a snorting noise that made Raquel laugh out loud.

"Let's get to work and put a call into G.G. If we get her voicemail, we can leave a message and call back later," Raquel suggested.

"My mother used to say, 'Familiarity breeds contempt.' Don't encourage this Theresa thing, please," Vic pleaded.

"Get over it. It's just one date, and they probably will never even go out again. Besides, I have a feeling this case will be over soon."

# CHAPTER 32

"Sorry, guys, but I tried. The Dominican police are coming up with lots of bullshit excuses and delays on the burlap bag forensics. I have a feeling they just can't deliver," Jack stated. He spoke to Vic and Raquel from police headquarters in Higuey, not far from Punta Cana, on Vic's cell phone speaker.

"All we want to know is if there were any markings on the bags that could lead us to their origin, and what, if anything, was carried in the burlap?" Vic blurted.

"May I make a suggestion?" Jack requested.

"All ears," Raquel followed.

"I think we need to get the bags to an American lab, or up to NYPD, or to some competent company to do a full analysis. Otherwise, we are spinning our wheels on arguably, the single most important piece of evidence we have in this case," Jack appealed.

"Vic, I agree. They just aren't set up for such a detailed analysis here. We spoke about calling G.G. I think we need to make that call right now," Raquel concurred.

"Okay. Jack, stay in Higuey. I'll get back to you soon. I'll get Fumar to release the bags to you and maybe get that jet so you can fly up to Virginia. It all depends if our friend at the Bureau will help. Sit tight."

Raquel immediately called and spoke with G.G., who agreed to set up a Skype call at her apartment. In ten minutes, they would see G.G. on Raquel's laptop.

"Hi, G.G. Long time!" Vic announced. He and Raquel were all smiles as if they were calling an old friend or relative. They had worked on the John Deegan case with G.G. for quite some time.

"Seven years," G.G. replied. Her face was deadpanned and haggard. G.G.'s hair looked like a rat's nest. The type that's found in the attic of an old Victorian house. She looked like she hadn't slept in days. Vic and Raquel could see a bit of G.G's apartment behind her. The place looked like Gail Gain was a compulsive hoarder. Huge piles of newspapers, books, empty soda bottles, and crushed packs of Pall Mall cigarettes littered the place.

"Time flies, I guess," Raquel muttered. G.G. seemed distracted. She lit a Pall Mall with a way too high flame on her lighter. That flame looked like it was coming off an industrial blow torch.

There was no friendly banter with G.G. She had an eccentric personality, was likely on the autism spectrum, perhaps Asperger's. It made her seem remote and unfriendly. G.G. wasn't about to ask how Vic and Raquel were doing or how the weather was. With G.G., there was only one thing on her mind. She is fixated on profiling and catching serial killers for the FBI.

"How have you been, G.G.?" Vic asked.

Gail just stared into the camera, her one eye going left, the other going slightly right. If Vic and Raquel didn't know the thirty-something woman had a 160 I.Q., they would have thought she was, at best, mildly mentally challenged. They waited on G.G. to snap out of her usual blank-staring trance.

G.G. suddenly spoke up, "Lewandowski sent me an e-mail a few days ago. He informed me you were on a serial case in the Dominican Republic." G.G.'s voice was so raspy, it sounded like she had been in the Sahara Desert for three days without water.

"Yes, we are in the Dominican, and we can use your help, G.G.," Vic disclosed.

"I don't fly!"

"Yes, we remember that. We are not asking for you to come here, we just need a little advice from you, and hopefully we will be able to apprehend this killer," Vic answered.

"Send an e-mail to me. I want as many specifications on the murder victims as possible."

"Not a problem. We are kind of pressed for time, G.G. Will you be able to look at this soon? We also have a few burlap bags, which were left on the heads of the four victims. We need them analyzed, post haste," Raquel declared.

G.G. gave no reply, just more staring.

"If we get those bags up to you, do you think it would help?" Vic inquired.

Another minute of staring and silence.

"Possibly." G.G. inhaled the cigarette deeply, letting the smoke billow out of her mouth and through her nose.

"We can send our man, Jack Nagle, with the bags tonight or first thing tomorrow morning. Will you be at headquarters?"

"No, I will be at the laboratory. I'm going there now. Send him there. Tell him not to try to shake my hand please. I don't like shaking hands."

"We remember that as well, G.G. Not to worry. So…we will e-mail to you the data on the victims immediately," Raquel articulated.

"Any suspects?" G.G. inquired. She was looking at her cigarette when she spoke.

"Yes, a few."

"Send that information to me." G.G. disconnected the Skype call.

"Jesus Christ! I can smell her through the video," Vic said.

"Oh, my God! I remember how badly she smelled. Why does the Bureau hold on to her?"

"Because she's a fucking real-deal genius, that's why."

# CHAPTER 33

"This is just like the one in Hollywood, Florida, Manny. It's fabulous," Theresa stated.

"Really? When did you go there?"

"Just last year with two of my girlfriends. We had an amazingly great time. It's called the Seminole Hard Rock. They have a huge casino, very much like this place, and an amazing hotel. It's amazing when three girls go to a casino, we never had to buy our own drinks. Guys kept buying round after round for us."

"I guess those guys have a good eye for pretty women," Manny uttered. *I wonder if she put out for any of those horny dudes?* he thought.

After driving around Punta Cana, seeing the sights, the beautiful beaches, and the coast line, then an exciting a two-hour, two-person, speedboat trip, the couple went to the Hard Rock Café for a late lunch.

"I hope you like what you saw today?" Manny asked.

"I loved it. I really like this country. Especially the people and the pace. It's really like paradise."

"Well, I hope you like me too, Theresa."

Manny was wondering all day when he would start to put his best moves on the hottie tutor. As they walked toward the bar, Manny put his arm around Theresa's thin waist.

"You're a great guy, Manny. And a wonderful tour guide."

"That's it? Just a great guy?" Manny stopped walking. He pulled Theresa closer to him, like he was trying to embrace her in an intimate dance. The teacher pulled away.

"What's wrong?" Manny asked.

"I had a great time with you today, Manny, but I don't want to turn this into something."

"I don't understand, Theresa. What do you mean by 'something'?"

"Look, I'm not looking to be another one of your conquests. The whole narrative disturbs me. The cliché of the American girl that screws the sexy Dominican guy on a first date. That's not me."

"See! You think I'm sexy. That's a start," Manny blurted. He wasn't joking.

"I'm getting very tired, and I don't want to take advantage of Raquel and Vic's good will. Anyway, I want to go back and take care of Gabriella before she goes to bed."

Manny persisted. His Latino macho ego was wounded. He pulled her close to him again. "Just one nice kiss?"

"No nice kiss. Now take me the fuck back to the White House," Theresa insisted. She was a New York City girl who took no bullshit from anyone, especially a pushy guy.

Manny stormed off like a petulant child, leaving Theresa to follow. The couple did not exchange another word for the twenty-minute ride back to Tortuga Bay.

"Hi, everyone, I'm back!" Theresa called out. Gabriella bounded down the staircase and jumped into her teacher's arms.

"I missed you Miss Panny...I really did!" Gabriella declared.

"Not as much as I missed you, Gabby." Theresa hugged her pupil, kissing her soft cheek.

Vic and Raquel were busy pouring over their notes on the case in the living room-turned war room. Vic still wanted nothing to do with the entire situation. He didn't miss a beat with the work. Raquel jumped from her chair to greet Theresa.

"I think we all missed you. Did you have a good time?" Raquel inquired.

"This whole area is lovely. Around Bavaro is a little seedy, and the zig-zagging mopeds and bikes are enough to make you dizzy, but the people are really sweet."

"You're home early. Did you eat?"

"Don't ask!" Theresa mumbled. Her face was red from the sun, but Raquel could tell she was pissed. "I'm starved!"

"Oh, boy…okay, do you mind leftovers? Chicken and rice and a nice salad? Louisa is in her room, but I'm sure she won't…"

"No, no…I can get it. Gabby, come and keep me company. Let me show you on the map where I went today. I'll tell you all about my boat trip and all the beautiful fish and coral I saw."

🗡 🗡 🗡

Raquel returned to the conference table and Vic. She decided not to say anything to Vic about Theresa's obvious annoyance. Raquel didn't want to hear any 'I told you so' lecture. Deep down, she knew Vic was right.

"Tomorrow morning, Jack is flying to Quantico. Fumar was totally cooperative. He also volunteered to go with me to visit Ralph Ledon. It's about time we follow up on that lead. It's a touchy situation, so we need to tip-toe around a bit," Vic announced.

"I'm going to work out a plan to get close to the Danish couple. Jimmy is out with Lenny right now figuring things out, and Lenny has already set the trap," Raquel offered.

"That leaves that groundskeeper, Freddy. I think we should assign Lieutenant Castillo to lead that investigation. Let's talk with him in the morning. Right now, I want to take my lovely Puerto Rican wife up to our suite and watch some television," Vic pronounced.

"Excuse me, Mr. Gonnella, but if you make a move to that remote control, I will stab you in your hand."

# CHAPTER 34

"Isabel, I heard from Lenny. He has an opportunity for us today while the kids are in school," Adam announced.

"Really? I must tell you, I'm very much in the mood, but I have a golf lesson at eleven," Adam's wife replied.

"From what Lenny said to me, it may be a good idea to cancel that lesson. I have tennis lessons to give from four to seven. We can easily be done by three, before the kids get home.

"Tell me more," Isabel blurted.

"Evidently, she is the most gorgeous Venezuelan he has seen so far. She just arrived in Punta Cana yesterday. Nineteen years old and kinky, he said. He can arrange her for us for two hundred American."

"Ask him to send a photo."

"I already did. We should be getting it by text in a few minutes."

In the Arrecife section of Punta Cana, a mere three-minute drive from the White House, Adam and Isabel Jensen lived in a luxury villa they managed for a wealthy family from Copenhagen. The handsome couple, both tall, Nordic blondes, had a penchant for exotic women who were willing to share their bed for money. Lenny had been with Isabel a few times while Adam took steamy home-made videos. Isabel liked girls as much as she liked men, while Adam was strictly a Latina lover.

Adam was the man that every single and married woman in Punta Cana desired. He was perfectly built with a gleaming white smile and longish blonde hair, which was indeed a rarity in the Dominican Republic. Isabel had the high cheek bones of an international fashion model and a body that betrayed having two children. She worked out with a personal trainer at their home every other day.

The Jensens had plenty of money from several luxury homes which they managed for their employers. Together, they enjoyed an enviable life and an open sexual relationship.

Adam's phone sounded a ding.

"Very nice…very, very nice," Adam spouted. He handed his phone to his eager spouse.

"Look at her lips. Her ass and legs are amazing," Isabel declared. She was staring at the photo of the girl with deep intent. "She is definitely high quality, that's for sure. Call Lenny back. I'm cancelling my lesson," Isabela blurted.

Fumar and Vic drove up to Ralph Ledon's sprawling mansion, which was high up on a hill and overlooked the Punta Espada Golf Club. They were driven in an official Ministry of Interior and Police vehicle, replete with the symbol of the Ministry on both front doors and official license plates on both ends.

"This is a very impressive villa," Vic spouted.

"What did you expect from the richest man in the region? Probably the entire country, maybe the entire Caribbean."

"This has to be a fifty-thousand square foot house, I bet."

"I've learned not to be impressed by things people have. A lot of rich people in this country have done a lot of crimes. I look at people as being all intrinsically evil. Ledon included," Fumar expressed.

"Raquel would call that jaded. I call it realistic. We think alike, my friend," Vic retorted.

Fumar and Vic walked to the massive oak front door from the driveway, made of pink, crushed coral stones and pebbles, then onto white and black marble tiles with gold inlays that resembled giant coffee beans. Fumar took his official hat off, tucked it under his left arm, and rang the bell. Vic stood aside from him, feeling like a delivery boy from the A&P in the Bronx.

"Good morning, may I help you, sir?" a butler answered. He had a British accent and the bad teeth to go along with it.

"Good morning, I am Lieutenant General Esteban Disla Martinez of the Identification and Investigation unit of the Ministry of Interior and

Police, and this is Mr. Vic Gonnella from New York City. We are here to pay a courtesy call on Mr. Ledon.

"Please come in, gentlemen. I will announce you to Mr. Ledon presently."

"I can live here…no problem," Vic mused aloud.

"I couldn't afford the wall paper," Fumar whispered. An unexpected bead of sweat ran down Fumar's neck, staining his light brown uniform shirt.

The two men looked around the foyer and at the triple marble staircase that ran up to the second floor, in wonderment. The crystal chandeliers were off, but multi-colored spotlights gave the place an almost garish appearance.

The butler returned quickly. Vic was too busy looking at the man's stained teeth to realize he was dressed in a formal morning suit, tails and all.

"Gentleman, Mr. Ledon will be down directly. He is finishing an overseas call. He's asked me to direct you to the fish pond beyond the pool area."

*Sounds like a fifteen-minute walk,* Vic thought as the two lawmen followed Ledon's domestic.

As they approached the pool, there she was, Lissandra-Hoyas Ledon, but this time she wasn't in a formal, white silk pantsuit. Lissandra was sitting up in a chaise longue under a flowing palm tree, wearing a pair of large sunglasses and the most incredible bikini either man ever had the good fortune to see. Her breasts filled out the skimpy gold top, plus a little extra on the sides. The bottom was nothing more than a sparkling gold G-string.

*Jesus Christ,* both men thought.

"Well, hello again, Mr. Gonnella!" Lissandra called out. She put her book down, stood from her seat, put her backless four-inch high heels on, and headed for the two men. Fumar, his job depending on decorum, looked around like he was a student of interior design. Vic enjoyed the entire floor show.

"I'm surprised and flattered that you even recall my name, Mrs. Ledon," Vic blubbered.

Lissandra approached Vic, kissing him on both cheeks. She formally introduced herself to the general with a strong handshake.

"Mr. Gonnella, my husband has taught me to remember names so I could do what I just did with you. I've trained myself to remember everyone I meet, it's like a game. And how is Raquel Ruiz?"

"Fantastic! I…I mean she is well, thank you. I was saying fantastic to complement your amazing memory."

"I assume you are here to see Ralph. He's had a very busy morning, just like every morning. I do know he is leaving for Cuba this afternoon for a few days," Lissandra disclosed. She removed her sunglasses, and her sparkling, black eyes betrayed an interest in Vic. Vic swallowed hard.

"Well, Mr. Gonnella, so nice to see you again, how is your stunning wife, Raquel?" Ralph Ledon shouted.

"See what I mean?" Lissandra whispered. Lissandra said her goodbyes. She shook Vic's hand, and held onto it a moment too long.

The two men shook hands. Ralph's handshake was like a vise. Vic introduced General Martinez using his full name. He surprised himself that he got the whole name right.

"What can I offer you gentlemen to drink?"

"Espresso, please, if it's not too much trouble," Vic said.

Ralph broke out in a loud, cackling laugh. "Mr. Gonnella, they don't call me the coffee king for nothing. Our espresso machine is the size of a Ford Taurus."

All three men got a good laugh at Ralph's analogy.

"And I have the proper liqueur to correct the coffee, as the Italians say. I assume, being Italian, you would prefer anisette?"

"Perfect…you could have said Sambuca," Vic was being his affable self.

"No red-blooded southern Italian would drink Sambuca with his coffee," Ralph laughed.

"And you, General? Anisette for you?"

"No, sir, sorry, just as it is."

"Ahhh, a true Latino. A man after my own heart."

A short, bald, uniformed waiter overheard the orders and moved quickly to fill them.

"Let's go to the fish pond. I like it out there," Ralph commanded.

The pond was three feet deep all around and as large as an Olympic swimming pool. Thousands of fish swam in the salt water with indigenous coral that was visible all the way to the pool's bottom.

"You know something, gentlemen? We are very much like those fish. They are all trying to survive in that pool and in the sea, just as we are. The only thing is, I'm not sure if they have feelings which interrupt their subsistence as humans do."

Fumar stepped up, "You pose an amazing philosophical question. Do fish have feelings? I am of the opinion that they do not. I believe they are commanded by nature for the sole purpose of procreation."

"Very interesting, General. I would like to spend more time philosophizing with a bright man like yourself, but I'm afraid I have to be out of the country for a few days. I'm leaving soon."

Fumar cleared his throat, "Allow me to get to the point of our visit, sir. I'm sure you are aware of the murders we have experienced of late here in Punta Cana."

"You mean the Butcher of Punta Cana? Yes, I am aware of this."

"Mr. Ledon, the women who were killed, they were all Venezuelan prostitutes. Their bodies have all been found within a six-kilometer distance from each other. As you likely know, one murdered girl was found right down there at Punta Espada," Fumar explained.

"Yes, I can see the cave where she was found from my upstairs balcony. Very distressing."

"Yes, sir, I'm sure. Have you taken any extra security precautions, Ralph?" Vic asked.

"Ahhh, I'm putting two and two together now. So, you are the famous American detective! You have been called in to help find the Butcher. Now I understand, and I am even more honored to have met you."

Vic smiled and bowed his head a bit.

"To answer your question, I have not increased security, and I'll tell you my thinking. Aside from an alarm system and some cameras around this place, Lissandra and I are championship marksmen. We compete at the gun club in La Romana. She can shoot the balls off a bee. I'm not so bad either. But more than anything, he is only killing Venezuelans. We, as everyone knows, are Cuban, and the last I looked, we are not prostitutes. So why be concerned?"

"At the risk of being rude, Ralph. If I gave you some dates, can you retrace your steps and tell us your whereabouts?" Vic pushed.

"What?" Ledon demanded. "So, I am a suspect in this shit? That is the most absurd thing I've ever heard! General, I am surprised that you would allow this kind of questioning, knowing my connections in La Capital and my stature in the country. I must be in a dream!"

"Mr. Ledon. Until we find this killer, this maniac, we have to investigate every lead," Fumar replied.

"Tell me how I came to be investigated, General?"

"Someone came forward and informed our task force that you often engage with prostitutes. With a special interest in Venezuelan prostitutes. We are simply following up on that assertion."

"Look it, if any cocksucker points a finger at a rich man, are you so gullible to believe it? What if I tell you that many of the leaders of your Dominican Republic go with prostitutes? Will you knock on their doors and accuse them of murder, too?"

"Ralph, no one is accusing you. We simply want to put all the pieces of this puzzle together. Your name came up, and as absurd as it sounds, we have a job to do. Tell us where you were on certain dates, and we will all move on," Vic implored.

"I have business in Cuba today. Send me the fucking dates, and I will speak with my lawyer, and he will let you know if I will play in your retarded game."

Vic and Fumar rose to leave the fish pond. Ralph stared at the fish, ignoring the two completely.

"Thank you, Mr. Ledon. I will be in contact by way of e-mail."

“And I will start fucking Brazilian chicas.”

As they left the coffee king’s villa, Fumar noticed a larger than normal, custom-made, four passenger golf cart parked just outside one of the four garages. The cart had some extras that were not usually seen on the golf courses. Four speaker stereo system, oversized halogen headlights, a fan on the driver and passenger side, and large tires with custom rims.

“Look at those tires,” Fumar whispered.

“I’ll get someone up here to take a look,” Vic stated.

“I should be saying that to you. I have an entire police department at my disposal,” Fumar said.

“Yeah, but I got the guy to handle this…trust me. He’s special.”

# CHAPTER 35

"Are you getting bored yet?" Vic asked. He called John Deegan on his cell.

"How can I be bored, watching you parade in and out of that White House you are staying at?" John Deegan replied.

"It's a bit weird having an escaped, international serial killer stalking my job, but we had such a great time the last few episodes, we may as well work together."

"Great! I have a job again!" Deegan shouted.

"Who said anything about a job? This is a favor, old timer."

"To me, it's still a job. Tell me, tell me, tell me."

"One of the suspects in the case, who happens to be one of the richest men in the DR, is Ralph Ledon. Do you know him?"

"I know of him, the coffee king. He's in the Forbes One Hundred, I recall."

"That's him. Filthy rich. I just want you to review the situation and do some stealth reconnaissance. Are you game?"

"Sure, I am. And I'll throw in a little more advice for you. I'll hold my thoughts for the lunch you're gonna buy me. But, my dear Gonnella, I'll be polite and hold my tongue, for now.

"Okay, Deegan, I would like you to..." Vic was cut off by Deegan.

"Tut, tut, tut...I already know what you need. I'll get the results to you in a day or so. I was thinking about looking into Ledon a few days ago. I just wanted the satisfaction of getting a call from you."

Deegan ended the call.

"Hello, Ms. Gain. I'm Jack Nagle." Jack was at the FBI forensics laboratory in Quantico, Virginia to bring the four sealed evidence bags containing the burlap bags found on the heads of the four murdered girls.

G.G. was in her small office, her desk so completely covered with papers, empty coffee cups, and Coca Cola cans that Jack could not tell if the desk was wood or metal.

*That smell is a combination of cigarette smoke and ass,* Jack said to himself.

G.G. looked up, her thick glasses on the bridge of her nose. She just stared up at the former Marine.

Jack stared back with an awkward pause.

"Don't worry, Ms. Gain, I don't like to shake hands either." Jack was attempting to win her over. To no avail.

"Do you have the burlap?"

"Yes, ma'am. They are in this bag, all sealed."

"You'll need a COC."

"Pardon?"

"A chain of custody form. I have one here somewhere."

G.G. began to rummage through the mess of papers until she found the document. Without looking up, G.G. offered the pre-signed form to Jack.

"You all know the perp is a mission serial killer, correct?" G.G. blurted.

"Ma'am?"

"You need to take notes from Mr. Gonnella. From what I have ascertained from the data that was sent to me, this killer falls into a mission-oriented murderer. I've eliminated the other categories from my profile." G.G was scratching her matted mane. Jack thought he saw dandruff falling onto the papers in front of her.

"Other categories?"

"Yes. The killer is not a lust nor power-control murderer. Nor is he a visionary or thrill killer. It's obvious to me that the perp is justifying his actions, thinking it's a necessity to remove these prostitutes from society.

He is likely selecting Venezuelan women to make a statement on the conditions in that country or perhaps from some deeply hidden guilt for using these women in his past. Rituals are performed after these kinds of murders. In this case, the mutilation is his ritual. He selects girls who look alike and feels they should be honored to be killed by him. It's a classic mission case. He will not stop until he is caught or killed."

"I see."

"I believe that this killer has a quota. Generally, ten to twelve murders. Remember, this is theoretical…hold on please."

G.G. took a crumpled pack of Pall Mall cigarettes, looking for a smoke. There were none in that pack, so she grabbed for a fresh one in a carton atop the mess of papers. She lit up, inhaling deeply, blowing a cloud of smoke into the air.

"I'm surprised you can smoke in here," Jack mentioned.

"Either I smoke, or I go home."

"I see. So, tell me, shall I stay around and wait for the analysis of the burlap?"

"Two-day process," G.G. muttered.

"I guess I'll head back to Punta Cana then."

G. G. went into one-minute stare mode.

"Suit yourself," G.G. muttered.

# CHAPTER 36

"So, what happened?" Raquel asked.

"I was having a great time all day. We did lots of stuff. Then we went to the Hard Rock to eat, and he turned a little creepy," Theresa responded.

Raquel was getting ready to go out in the field with Jimmy to do surveillance on the Jensens. She stopped to see Gabriella, who was doing a math recitation. Theresa and Raquel stepped away for a few minutes.

"Really creepy or just creepy?" Raquel inquired.

"I'll put it to you this way, he was pushy, then he wouldn't take no for an answer. I told him in no uncertain terms, I'm not that girl."

"He has that look. He probably hasn't heard the word 'no' very often down here."

"He drove me back here from Bavaro, as if acting like a baby would possibly change my mind. Before that, he was a gentleman."

"I'm a bit surprised at him, knowing that you are with us, but you know about Latin men and their overactive testosterone."

"Yeah, he's gorgeous and he knows it, but now it's going to be a bit awkward if he comes here for a meeting."

"I'll keep an eye on him. Just go about your business and ignore him."

"My intention exactly."

On the way to the Jensens' Arrecife villa, Jimmy filled Raquel in on the plan.

"Lenny got it done. These two Jensen characters are maybe the most messed up couple in the Caribbean. The Venezuelan girl's name is Cynthia, and she is a starlet, very young and very gorgeous. Isabel Jensen runs the show over there, and she's a total freak," Jimmy advised.

"How young?" Raquel inquired.

"Nineteen. She got here yesterday from Caracas. Lenny will be bringing her inside."

Jimmy continued, "She's all set. I have a wireless recorder in her bag, one inside the lining of her jeans, and one in her cell phone. Obviously, she has no idea why we want this, but money talks."

"What time are they arriving?"

"At eleven. Fifteen minutes. I have two of Fumar's detectives in a villa across the street, dressed as laborers. They are picking weeds and pruning trees. There's another two men backing us up in a truck in front of the house next door. We will be a few yards away, ready to pounce if we think the girl is in any real danger."

"What about Lenny?"

"Not sure yet. If the Jensens want him to film them with the girl, which they have done before, he stays. If not, he'll be sitting out here with us.

"Do we totally trust Lenny?" Raquel asked. She crinkled her face and shook her head slightly.

"He's a dog, but he knows Fumar will lock his ass up. These Dominican prisons are what nightmares are made of, Raquel, and Lenny has only one shot, and that's to cooperate. If he double deals us, he's fucked. Pardon the pun."

Jimmy coasted up to the front of the villa next to the Jensens. It was a few minutes to eleven when Lenny showed up with Cynthia.

Gorgeous was an understatement. Cynthia was a bit taller than most of the Venezuelan chicas they saw, with long, straight, black hair that went to the top of her perfectly-shaped butt. She wore a one-piece, cream-colored, spandex jumpsuit that molded up her butt crack. The top portion of the jumpsuit would have exposed her perfectly-formed young breasts, save for double-sided tape on each tit. A pair of four-inch red heels and a brown Louis Vuitton clutch finished her look.

"Jesus Christ!" Raquel gasped.

"Told ya!" Jimmy offered.

"Why does a woman who looks like that need to sell herself to these fucking people?"

"Just do the math, Raquel."

"I mean she can have any rich neurosurgeon in the New York tri-state area."

"Or an old retired cop like me," Jimmy added. He was daydreaming while he followed her ass into the villa. Lenny took a quick look toward the vehicle Jimmy and Raquel were in.

"You're packing, right?" Raquel asked.

"Fuckin A. And here's a little friend for you, just in case," Jimmy added. He reached under the car's seat, handing Raquel a gray, nine millimeter Beretta APX sub-compact.

"Now I'm comfortable," Raquel muttered.

"Hola, Adam, hola Isabel, this is Cynthia," Lenny announced.

Cynthia held out her hand to Adam. He took her hand and kissed it gently. The chica then offered to shake Isabel's hand. Mrs. Jensen moved past the young woman's arm and moved in for an erotic kiss. Cynthia got right into the girl-on-girl action. Isabel was like a German Shepherd in heat. She wrapped her leg around the chica and started to hump.

Lenny was sent on his way. A possible sign that the Jensen's didn't want any witness. Lenny retreated to the vehicle with Jimmy and Raquel as planned. In typical NYPD style, Jimmy frisked the Dominican before allowing him in the vehicle.

It wasn't long before they were in the master suite. Lenny had to translate for Jimmy as the voices came over the receiver.

Isabel was the director. "Put your mouth here, your pussy there, sit on his face while I kiss you. Get into this position, hang off the bed a little, put this inside me, do you like it baby?" Mostly moaning and short sentences of instruction were enough to get Lenny and Jimmy aroused. Raquel was feigning disgust, but she was getting moist visualizing the action.

The action lasted until about two-thirty. There were only pleasurable moans. No choking, no hitting, not even an ass was slapped. Just a pure, wholesome threesome.

"That was a pleasant afternoon, I guess?" Jimmy uttered.

"Scratch those two off the list, Jimmy," Raquel said.

# CHAPTER 37

Lieutenant Castillo was called to the White House for a meeting with Fumar, Vic, and Raquel.

"Castillo, the last assignment given to you was for information and analysis on the burlap bags. You came up short on this, to my dismay. It's embarrassing enough that our department was inept on the murder scenes and forensics. Not to be able to find the origins of the burlap reflects poorly on our entire operation. Mr. Gonnella and Ms. Ruiz have sent their man to Washington with the bags. It will be another few days before we get the results. In that time, if there is another homicide...well...both of us may be reassigned. But of course, you have the political contacts to put yourself anywhere you desire," Fumar stated. His manner was both rude and sarcastic.

"General, I take total responsibility for that delay and failure. As you are aware, our department is limited in many ways, but as the assignment was mine alone, I should have made other arrangements with the bags. If I may speak freely, sir, I will not use my father's contacts to hide behind my failures. If need be, I will resign my commission should my inaction result in another death."

"There is no need for that, Lieutenant. We already have another assignment for you. One that needs complete discretion and immediate action. I will leave the details of this assignment to Mr. Gonnella and Ms. Ruiz."

"Lieutenant, I find it admirable that you are man enough not to throw your department under the bus, as we say in the States. Let's just move forward, please," Vic declared.

"Thank you, sir."

Raquel chimed in. "While we await the analysis from our FBI forensic lab, assuming that they actually come up with an answer, there are two things on our list, right on that whiteboard, that we need to dive into. Someone said that a few uses for burlap are coffee and landscaping. One of our suspects, as you know, is the coffee king. The other, who we have not investigated so far, is a landscaper. Namely, Fernando "Freddy" Reyes."

Vic continued, "We need you to do an in-depth investigation on this Freddy guy. I don't mean calling him in and beating the crap out of him.

I'm talking about an old-fashioned detective job. One of the Venezuelan prostitutes had an experience with him,, and if we are to believe her, he illustrated a violent tendency that does not preclude him from being a killer.

"I will give you her testimony on Reyes, and we can bring the accuser to the table if need be. In the meantime, we want to find out everything we can on this guy. Ex-wives, old girlfriends, guy friends, his job at Punta Espada, his landscaping business, does he use prostitutes, anything and everything," Vic verbalized.

"Are you up for this assignment, Lieutenant?" Raquel asked.

"Yes, ma'am. I'm honored to do this investigation."

Fumar cleared his throat. He removed his ever-present, unlit cigar from his mouth.

"Lieutenant, I don't have to explain the importance of this assignment. You have my complete support, and you have carte blanche for anything you need within our department."

"Thank you, General. I will do my best!" Castillo exclaimed.

Castillo saluted his General and shook hands with Vic and Raquel. As he was walking toward the front door, a familiar voice came from behind him.

"You are very impressive, Lieutenant. I couldn't help but overhear what was going on. I wasn't eavesdropping, mind you," Theresa said.

The tutor was sitting with Gabriella in the dining room next to the war room. Gabriella was reading an assignment. Theresa made her way toward the foyer to speak with Castillo.

"Why, thank you, ma'am. That is very kind of you to say." Castillo took his hat off and tucked it under his left arm.

"I must tell you, Gabriella has not let your grandmother's doll out of her sight. That was so very generous of you."

“I’m so happy about that, Ms. Panny. I love children. Not having any of my own, and no prospects, I thought perhaps she would like the gift.”

“No prospects? A man with your position should have a line of women to choose from,” Theresa replied.

“Well…I… my job takes most of my time. And frankly, I’m a bit…how can I say this…?”

“Shy? Reserved?”

“I prefer reserved,” Castillo uttered. He looked down at his shoes, blushing just a bit.

“Lieutenant, that is an admirable trait. I prefer people who are a bit reserved over people who are overly aggressive. Men and women alike.”

“Thank you, Ms. Panny, I must be on my way.”

“Please, call me Theresa. May I call you Mateo?

“Mateo or Matt, please do. Thank you. Hope to see you again,” Castillo answered. He wanted to say more, but didn’t know how.

“It would be my great pleasure to see you again, Mateo,” Theresa replied.

# CHAPTER 38

"Top of the mornin' to you, good sir. Is there a chance I can have a word with the master of this fine house?" John Deegan asked. He used his family's original Donegal Irish brogue to mask his real New York accent.

"May I ask who is calling?" the butler asked. Hearing the accent, the English butler looked the caller up and down, turning up his nose to indicate his displeasure. *Bloody wanker,* he thought.

Deegan craned his neck, feigning soreness to take a peek inside the villa. The butler closed the door behind him to prevent the Irishman's curiosity.

"Me name is Sean. Sean Collins from Nova Publishing, Dublin." Deegan flashed a counterfeit, yet official-looking, I.D. card, his picture prominent in the center.

"And the purpose of your visit?" the butler asked through his messy teeth and tight jaw.

"I'm a photographer for Architecture Ireland. A wee magazine for the trade back home."

Deegan wore a wrinkled pair of brown Bermuda shorts, a short-sleeved, green rugby shirt, white socks under sandals, topped off by an Irish tweed flat cap. Two, thirty-five millimeter cameras hung from his neck, covering each side of his chest, one a Canon, the other made by Nikon. He carried a small backpack with various photography items inside.

"I don't believe the master is available. What can I do for you, sir?" The "sir" was dripping in British sarcasm.

"I've been sent to the Dominican to photograph some of the better homes for the magazine. I'm sure ya heard of Architecture Ireland." Deegan put his right hand to his mouth, covering it like he was sharing secret, "And to play a wee bit of golf on the company."

"Kindly leave your card, Mr. Collins, and when the master is available, perhaps he will ring you."

"Oh, Jesus, don't ya know, I'm to leave in the morn' for Shannon, and I wouldn't want our readers to miss what I've seen here, simply the best villa on the whole island. Maybe in all the Caribbean, fer fook's sake."

"Sorry, my good man. Perhaps you should have called ahead and made an appointment."

"Give a fella a break, will ya? I can take a few shots of the exterior and be on me way. I'll be gone before ya can even count to twenty."

Lissandra was curious who rang the bell. She opened the door wide and stepped out onto the marble walk. Deegan's knees almost buckled. Lissandra was wearing a blue cover-up over her white, string bikini.

"Henry, who is this?" Lissandra queried.

"No matter, madam. He is looking to take some photos for a bloody Irish magazine."

"Isn't that special! Our home in a magazine in Europe? Let him in, Henry."

"This is quite out of the ordinary, madam," Henry protested.

"Don't be silly. We will be the talk of Ireland, and who knows where else?"

Henry, the butler, was quietly snarling like a badger.

"Well thank you, madam. Me wife is expecting me back tomorrow for our anniversary. This is me final assignment, don't ya know! They have me pensioned off after this shoot. I've been dodging retirement for a good ten years. Me boss says I should give another guy a chance. He says I must have me first communion money wrapped inside me baptismal money. Me name is Sean Collins, I'm delighted to meet ya, madam."

"What a sweet man. I'm sure your wife is happy you are returning. Bring her something nice from Punta Cana," Lissandra declared.

"Indeed I will, missus, indeed I will."

"Would you like interior shots as well, Mr. Collins?"

"If it's not putting ya out, missus."

Henry followed behind Deegan everywhere he and Lissandra went. The bedroom suites, the marble staircase, the pool area, the wine cellar, the billiard room, as Deegan clicked away. Only Ralph Ledon's study was locked and off limits.

"Mother of Jesus, would ya look at that machine? Is it for coffee, missus?" Deegan asked. The machine is in the massive kitchen, which dwarfed the three of them.

"Yes, only Cuban coffee is served here. My husband made his fortune in the coffee business. This coffee maker is one of a kind, custom made for him. It's his pride and joy."

"Look at all the contraptions and steamers and pipes an' things. Would I be imposing to ask for a wee taste of coffee from that goliath?" Deegan spotted something near the coffee machine that peaked his interest.

"I am so sorry, Mr. Collins, I am such a terrible host. I was just excited to have photos taken of the villa. Henry, please make us each a café Cubano," Lissandra ordered.

Henry would have preferred to get a root canal on his front snaggle-tooth.

Deegan snapped away from camera to camera like a Japanese tourist. Lissandra and Deegan had two coffees each and chatted about the home and her former life in Cuba.

"You were born in Cuba, then?" Deegan inquired.

"Yes, I was. I learned English from my parents who spoke it fluently. I look around this place, and I have to pinch myself sometimes. Our house in Cuba was no more than a shack made of tin with seven people, one bedroom, and a toilet outside. I don't think I've seen all the bathrooms in this villa," Lissandra chuckled.

"Well that's progress fer ya."

Deegan offered his humble gratitude for the photo session and the coffee.

"Missus, thanks fer the wonderful tour and fer allowing me to shoot yer beauteous villa. If I can get yer e-mail address, I'll send them off to ya when I'm back in the ol' sod, then in the fall, a copy of the magazine will arrive in yer post."

Lissandra and Henry saw Deegan to the door.

“One more set of photos on the front exterior will wrap it up. Yer as kind as yer beautiful, missus.”

Lissandra kissed Deegan on his cheek for the compliment. Henry and she retreated inside the villa.

Deegan was chomping at the bit. He had only one more thing he needed to photograph. Luckily, the garage door was open.

# CHAPTER 39

"Martinez, have you no brains? Do you have any idea who Ralph Ledon is? I just came from the President's office. He has heard from Ledon and his fucking lawyer. Do you have even one clue as to how much support he gives to this administration?" Minister Castillo screamed.

"Minister Castillo, we are doing a legitimate murder investigation. Information that has been brought to us indicates that Ledon may be a suspect," Fumar replied. He was sitting with Vic and Raquel in the war room planning their next moves.

"Do you mean to imply that the richest man in this country is killing foreign prostitutes just for fun?"

"Minister, it is incumbent upon me to follow each and every lead. I must tell you, we are awaiting more solid evidence on Mr. Ledon. I am not ruling out anything in this case. You yourself have indicated the damage that these murders can hurt our tourist economy. If Mr. Ledon is cleared of any wrongdoing based on evidence, I will apologize to him myself."

"Is this the best you have? What is Gonnella saying about this ridiculous assertion?"

"I am with Mr. Gonnella and Ms. Ruiz now. They are supporting my action on Mr. Ledon without reservation; however, the responsibility of this case rests with me. All we simply asked of Mr. Ledon is that he should tell us his whereabouts on the days these murders occurred. I don't believe he should be given any preferential treatment in this case."

"There is a word called discretion. You lacked discretion in this instance. Perhaps you should have contacted me to discuss Mr. Ledon before you approached him," Minister Castillo shouted.

"And if I had? You would have ordered me not to visit him, that is now obvious to me."

"I will tell you in no uncertain terms, Ledon is not to be disturbed. That is a direct order!"

Minister Castillo hung up on Fumar.

Vic had no idea what was going on, but Raquel understood Fumar's part of the conversation.

"What the hell's going on?" Vic inquired.

"I've just been ordered to stay away from Ralph Ledon from Minister Castillo...that prick!"

"Amazing! Money talks just like in the States," Vic replied.

"I swear on everything I love, if the evidence points to this coffee king, I will put the cuffs on him myself. I hope to God he is the Butcher, I hope..."

Raquel interrupted Fumar's thought, "Let's just see how things play out. Right now, we play it their way. If anything comes up that points directly at Ledon, we will cross that bridge when we come to it."

"She's right. Let's see what happens," Vic agreed.

# CHAPTER 40

"Not one blemish on his record. Nothing! This guy is as clean as can be. We trailed him for two days. He goes to the golf course at five-thirty or six in the morning, works all day, then he stops at his villa accounts to see the work his crew did that day, goes to eat dinner, alone, and goes home. His life seems very much just about his work and his business," Lieutenant Castillo reported.

"So, there is no violence reported in his record?" Fumar asked.

"Sir, he has no record. So far, the only thing that has led us to investigate him is an incident with a prostitute, that may or may not be true, the word of a known drug dealer and rapist, and the fact the he has access to burlap. As far as using prostitutes for his sex life, this isn't enough for us to assume he is a killer. Of course, we will continue to monitor his behavior around the clock. I'm simply reporting what had transpired over the past two days, General," Castillo stated.

"Lieutenant, keep on it, please. A serial killer is a very different and very difficult personality to figure out. Right now, he is still high on our list of potential killers. Let me state that the woman who reported him to us is credible. Just because she is a prostitute does not mean she wasn't a victim of his violent behavior," Raquel replied.

"Yes, ma'am."

Vic stepped in. "Have you ever heard of Ted Bundy, Lieutenant?"

"Yes, sir, I have. He was a serial killer in the United States."

"Well, he confessed to killing thirty women, but we will never know how many people he actually murdered. He was a good student, went to church, had a juvenile record for stealing that was erased when he turned eighteen, but no other police record. He was a very bright and articulate charmer and a madman at the same time. My point is, Lieutenant, that Fernando Reyes can very well be your country's Ted Bundy," Vic added.

"I understand, sir. I was merely reporting my findings, but in no way will I shirk my responsibilities. We will continue the investigation and surveillance."

"Look, we are all frustrated with this investigation. Just stay with it, Lieutenant," Raquel replied, "We'll catch whoever is responsible for this."

"Deegan here! Reporting to central!"

"What do you have, John?" Vic asked.

"I have plenty, my old friend. How about you and the lovely Raquel meet me somewhere? I'm starved, if you want to know the truth."

"There is a restaurant, Playa Blanca, on the beach. How about thirty minutes?" Vic asked.

"How about fifteen?"

"Always negotiating! On our way," Vic replied.

When Vic and Raquel arrived at the Playa, Deegan was sitting at a table under a palm tree in shorts, no shoes, a straw hat on his head, and an open, pinstripe Yankee shirt with MANTLE printed on the back.

"Nice shirt," Vic muttered.

"Great player. He was my idol when I was a kid in the Bronx. That's how old I am. Raquel, you look wonderful, a bit tired, but wonderful nonetheless," Deegan stated.

"Thank you, John. This case is giving me gray hair."

"I ordered some grilled local fish and some rice and beans. Unless you two have gone vegan on me," Deegan blurted.

"That's fine…what did you find out?"

"I can show you the photos I took."

"Photos?" Raquel asked.

"That Lissandra is such a nice lady. I even had a couple of coffees with her in the kitchen." John laughed.

"How the hell did you get inside that place?" Vic queried.

"I'm a bit of a wee charmer is all," Deegan used his brogue for effect.

"Jesus Christ! I'm afraid to ask," Vic responded.

Deegan took his cameras from a beach bag he had under his chair. He turned the Nikon on, and the viewfinder blinked on.

"Look at the size of their bedroom. It's two times bigger than my first apartment," Deegan said.

"C'mon, John, get to the point, will ya?" Raquel roared.

"Okay, so I'll bypass all of these then." Deegan flipped through the hundreds of photos until he found what he was looking for.

"Look at the size of that coffee machine, will ya?" Deegan blurted.

"How did you get her to be in the shot?" Raquel asked.

"Tell a woman she will be in a magazine, and she'll do anything," Deegan replied.

"Okay, so what's the big deal?" Vic inquired.

"Take your eyes of Lissandra and look to the right a bit?" Deegan recommended.

"Of course…burlap bags!" Raquel yelled. "I was looking at her outfit, too."

"Indeed, but when you are doing stealth work, you need to see everything!" Deegan preached.

"Are they the same type that were found on the bodies?" Raquel asked.

"Don't know that. If I was perfect, I would have grabbed one, but there were coffee beans in them and a fucking Brit asshole breathing down my neck," John added.

"I met that mutt when we interviewed Ledon. But Ledon is off limits now," Vic stated.

"What the hell do you mean, off limits?"

"John, this guy is mega rich. We asked him a few questions, you know, about where he was when the girls were killed, he freaked out on me and the general, then he ran to his friends in high places. He is not to be bothered," Vic explained.

"Okay, then. I guess I won't show you the two important photos I have in my other camera. No problem, I'll just keep them as a souvenir."

"Let's see 'em, Deegan," Raquel replied. Deegan loved games more than anything.

Deegan took out the Canon camera, set it on the table so the three of them could view the pictures together, and began to flick through the photos.

"There is the pool, nice pool, there is the backyard, nice grass, there are the rose bushes, nice thorns, there is the fish pool…did you two not notice anything?"

Vic and Raquel looked at each other for help. They shrugged their shoulders at one another.

"You guys disappoint me, really and truly, you do."

"What? What did we miss? Show them again," Raquel demanded.

"I only got a moment's glance, and I saw it right off. Maybe ya had to be there, I guess. Okay, I'll show only one shot."

Deegan scrolled to the photo he was talking about.

"It's the backyard lawn. It's a nice, full, Bermuda grass lawn," Vic said.

"Correctamundo, paisano. Look closer, if you will."

"I just see grass!" Raquel declared.

"Victor? One more try, for the daily double?"

"Beats the shit out of me," Vic answered.

Deegan took his pinky finger and pointed at the camera's screen.

"See it? Right there. Look at the difference in the color of the grass. That grass looks like it had something sprayed on it. Something gloopy that stuck to it and discolored it."

"Blood? Do you think it's blood?" Raquel spoke just above a whisper.

"Possibly. Just a theory I'm working on. Just a theory, but I have one more photo that needs comparative analysis. Let me bring it up." Deegan scrolled again. "Bingo."

"I saw that golf cart up at Ledon's villa. That's what I wanted you to look at," Vic almost shouted.

"I did better than look. I took a close-up of the tires. Compare this to the impressions we have. Let's see what happens at that point," Deegan pronounced.

Deegan sat back in his chair, a grin on his face, like an eight-year-old schoolboy who just gave the correct answer in a spelling bee.

Deegan jumped to his feet, startling Vic and Raquel. "Oh, my goodness. The fish is here! I'll fillet it for us. Vic, order a bottle of white, please."

# CHAPTER 41

"Hi, Ms. Gain. It's Jack Nagle, how are you? I'm back here in the Dominican Republic with Vic Gonnella and Raquel Ruiz. Can you see us?" The Skype reception was amazingly clear for the Dominican Republic.

Silence. G.G. picked at her teeth with a bent-open paper clip.

"Ms. Gain?"

"Yes. Speaking."

"Hello, G.G., its Vic," Vic almost laughed at how much like a mad scientist Gail Gain appeared.

Silence. G.G. began twirling a piece of her matted hair which hung past her Rosacea-ridden forehead.

"G.G., hi, it's Raquel. We called to find out if there are any results on the testing of the burlap bags."

G.G. lit a cigarette, spit out a piece of the tobacco from the unfiltered Pall Mall, took a sip of Pepsi, and coughed.

"I'm reviewing the final reports right now. The process is quite simple. We did trace evidence analysis on all four bags. Trace evidence analysis means exactly like what it sounds. There is a trace of matter attached to the Jute fibers of the burlap. From these strands, fiber testing is done using high-powered comparison microscopes, in this case, our laboratory utilized a Steindorff S-1010 Forensic Comparison Microscope.

Chemical analysis is then utilized. An electron microscope is the best instrument available to us to examine the surface of any fiber. With electron microscopy, a dry specimen can be easily examined so long as the thinness of the specimen is within a certain tolerance. The major limitation is that the specimen must be in a vacuum. So, in elementary terms, a beam of electrons is generated by a suitable, fixed source. That beam then scans the surface of the specimen, and remember, the specimen must be very thin, in some cases unweighable. Keep in mind, our technicians are trained at contamination identification by combining sample manipulation, hot stage microscope infrared, to determine the chemical composition of the fiber. The resulting data can then be utilized to trace the product back to the manufacturer using standard databases. This method enhances the probative value of the evidence."

"Excuse me, Ms. Gain?" Jack murmured.

"Please let me finish." G.G. scratched the back of her head like a flea-bitten dog. Raquel had to resist vomiting.

"Please keep in mind that scanning electron microscopy provides high-resolution and high depth-of-field images of the sample surface and near-surface. SEM is the most widely used analytical tool due to the extremely detailed images it can quickly provide. Combined with an auxiliary energy dispersive x-ray spectroscopy detector, SEM offers elemental analysis of nearly the entire periodic table."

"Ms. Gain!" Jack shouted.

"Speaking," G.G. replied. She never looked up at the Skype camera.

Vic jumped in, "G.G. we very much appreciate the detailed information and the favor you have given to us, but we are calling simply for the test results. As you know, this may be the best evidence we have in this case. The details can definitely be used later in court if need be."

"Court? Down in the Dominican Republic?" G.G. asked. She stared up at the ceiling with a look like a scared rabbit.

"Perhaps, assuming we apprehend the killer and get that far," Vic answered.

"I don't fly!" G.G. muttered.

"Don't be concerned about that, G.G. It's not like court in the States. Your written report will suffice."

"Coffee bean residue," G.G. blurted.

"Pardon me?" Vic queried.

"All four bags carried coffee beans at some point. There were trace amounts of paint on at least two of the bags. Perhaps some identification markings that were likely removed chemically."

Vic looked at Raquel and raised his eyebrows. He mouthed, "Ralph Ledon!"

"Thank you so much, G.G. This narrows down the field considerably. Anything else you can tell us?"

"Yes. There are burlap bags manufactured all over the world, Brazil, Uganda, Vietnam, the States. These bags were manufactured on the island of Cuba."

# CHAPTER 42

Vic immediately called Fumar, asking him to come to the White House for an important update.

"Fumar, are you close by?" Vic asked.

"Five minutes away, my friend. What's wrong?"

"Good, we have some interesting news. I'll wait for you to get here," Vic ended the call.

"Honey, call Jimmy Martin. He needs to be here," Vic asked his lady.

"This is turning out to be quite a ride. I hate to say it, but if Ralph Ledon is indeed a viable suspect, that news will bring the international media organizations flocking to Punta Cana. We better make sure we are right before anything leaks. If we are wrong, we will be the smacked ass of the entire world," Vic added.

Theresa, Gabriella, and Olga came into the war room.

"Look at how pretty you look!" Vic bellowed.

"Thank you, daddy," Gabriella replied. She was wearing a cute, pink sundress with white sandals and a bougainvillea corsage in her long, brown hair.

"Where are you guys going?" Raquel asked. Gabriella went to her mother, hugging her as Raquel stroked her hair.

"Don't you remember, today's the day we are going to the Bavaro Adventure Park," Theresa explained.

"Geez, I'm sorry. It totally slipped my mind with all that's going on," Raquel said.

"Mommy, daddy, they have an outdoor playground with lots of rides, rock climbing for kids, a big waterfall pool, and even buggy rides!" Gabriella exclaimed.

"I have her bathing suit on underneath her dress. And our own towels in this beach bag," Olga offered.

"Have fun, sweetie," Vic said, kissing his daughter's cheek.

"Listen, stay close to your abuelita and Miss Panny," Raquel warned.

"Not to worry, two detectives are driving us to the park. They will stay with us all day. We'll be back in time for dinner," Theresa replied.

Gabriella ran for the door just as Fumar and his aides arrived.

"We're going to the park in Bavaro," Gabriella announced.

Fumar took the cigar from his mouth and smiled from ear-to-ear.

"That's a great place. I took my children there many times. You will have great fun," Fumar added.

The general looked at the two detectives who were waiting outside in the Escalade. He pointed to Gabriella and put two fingers up to his eyes.

"Of course, General," one of the men responded. The three ladies loaded into the vehicle, and off they went.

"Fumar, we heard from the FBI lab. The analysis showed the burlap bags had remnants of coffee beans," Vic blurted.

"Son-of-a-bitch!" Fumar responded. His cigar almost fell from his mouth.

"And the bags are Cuban made," Raquel added.

"That's the smoking gun, don't you think?" Fumar declared.

"There's more," Vic stated. "The golf cart at the Ledon villa? The tire treads match the photos we have from one of the murder scenes. The last one on the beach where the victim was found in the boat."

"There is some possible evidence of blood on the back lawn at the villa, though we don't have samples of the grass. All we have in this regard are some photographs which indicate stains," Raquel added.

"May I ask how you came up with this information on the Ledon villa?" Fumar queried.

"Let's just say we have a special assistant who was able to get into the house and the surroundings," Vic stated.

"Mother of Jesus. Now what?" Fumar uttered. The general began to pace the floor, deep in thought. He lit his cigar even though he was inside the house.

"With your order to stay clear of Ledon, we have to be very cautious with our next steps," Raquel stated.

"I didn't obey my orders completely. I have a man in Havana trailing that coffee king bastard. He is still in Cuba," Fumar smiled.

"Good for you. I suggest we bring Lieutenant Castillo here. We can debrief him on Freddy Reyes. See where his investigation is going and brief him on the lab findings. I have a feeling we should not inform Sergeant Lopez," Vic cautioned.

"I agree totally. Lopez is a political climber like his father. I don't trust Lopez. Not in the least. If he knows about your findings, within an hour, I will be summoned to La Capital," Fumar seethed.

"My take as well. At some point, we will have to bring the evidence to Minister Castillo. I will lead the charge on that to keep you insulated from the politics," Vic declared.

"What in God's name would compel Ledon, a man with great wealth and power, with everything a man could want…what would make him kill these prostitutes?"

"If he is indeed the Butcher of Punta Cana, and should he be a classic, mission-oriented serial killer, perhaps there was something from his childhood that sparked that abnormal behavior. Or something else. Perhaps a religious fervor that wants him to eradicate prostitutes. Perhaps some form of guilt for having sex with them. There was really no sexual evidence on the bodies other than the mutilations, so it points to a mission, without a doubt," Raquel answered.

"And his use of prostitutes, with the gorgeous, young wife, leads one to assume he also has a sexual deviation, which puts him into an additional category of serial killer. A lust or thrill killer, in his own sick way," Vic added.

"Vic, I would love to get some hard samples of what we think may be blood on that lawn. Perhaps our friend can get back in there and pull some grass and dirt?" Raquel asked.

"Great idea. I'll reach out in a few. In the meantime, we need to put a soft surveillance on that villa. Fumar, can you get that done?"

"Absolutely. I'll get on it."

# CHAPTER 43

Lieutenant Castillo arrived at the White House within ten minutes of the call from his boss.

"What do you have to tell us about your investigation into Freddy Reyes, Lieutenant?" Fumar asked. They were sitting out on the veranda by the pool now. Fumar realized he was smoking inside the villa. His lighting up inside caused him to apologize to Raquel four times. Raquel graciously explained to the general that while growing up in the Bronx, her late father, her uncles, and her aunts all smoked in their homes. Cigars, cigarettes, and pipes were constantly lit in their small apartments with no thought of the odor or health issues. Fumar was relieved, as he grew up the same.

"General, this guy leads a very boring life so far. While we were snooping around and asking questions, we have discovered the staff and the workers, who maintain the golf course at Punta Espada and La Cana golf club, think Reyes is a good boss and a fair man. We have eyes on him twenty-four/seven. If he does anything, our men will know about it. Today is Friday. If he makes any crazy moves tonight, we will be all over him," Lieutenant Castillo reported.

"Are you satisfied with the men you have on Reyes?" Fumar asked.

"Yes, sir, they are all well trained, my best men."

Fumar looked approvingly, as if the discussion had been planned, at Vic and Raquel.

"Lieutenant, we have information, not yet totally conclusive, that Ralph Ledon is a key suspect in this case," Raquel offered.

Fumar spoke to his officer differently than ever before. A bit more like a partner rather than simply a subordinate. "Castillo, as you know, I've been ordered to stand down from Ledon. I am not to approach him or otherwise bother him. I trust you, Lieutenant. I know your dedication to this case will not bring you to contact your uncle or anyone else in La Capital. I will ask again for your total discretion and secrecy."

"You have my word, General. In case you haven't noticed, my uncle is not very kind to me. Never has been. Frankly, my father and the minister haven't spoken in many years. Political difference."

"I understand. That being said, I want you to keep close to me, if and when we need to move on Ledon. For the time being, please have your men report their findings to you on Reyes via telephone. And another important matter. I want Sergeant Lopez to be kept out of the loop on all matters surrounding this case. I will reassign him away from here as soon as I see the opportunity," Fumar stated.

"Yes, sir. I understand." Castillo couldn't help but feel pleased about Lopez's fall from grace. He never trusted the sergeant, with his caustic, sarcastic personality. In a way, Castillo was relieved not to have Lopez looking over his shoulder.

Vic jumped in, "Fumar, what are your plans with Dr. Fishman and Lenny? They have been locked up for a while now."

"I want to keep them on ice for a while. Ledon has a big reach everywhere in this country. If he thinks we have eliminated these two as suspects, perhaps he will get a bit nervous. They will stay in protective custody for the time being. Remember, our laws for detaining suspects are a bit different than yours," Fumar advised.

"But Ledon is still in Havana, correct?" Raquel asked.

"He is, and all indications are that he will remain there for a few more days."

The next three hours at the White House were spent entirely at the whiteboard. Lieutenant Castillo was briefed on the findings surrounding Ralph Ledon. Vic and Raquel summarized the entire case with Castillo and Fumar. The four law enforcement associates virtually eliminated Fishman, Lenny, and the Jensens as suspects. They were deemed as a sex deviate, a street thug, and kinky, in that order. All three did not fit the serial killer profile, and there was no real evidence indicating they murdered the four Venezuelan girls.

At the Bavaro Adventure Park, Gabriella was like a whirling dervish, going from ride-to-ride, then from the waterfall pool to the buggies. The park was crowded with school kids, teachers, and parents. A few of the more popular rides like the whip and the go-carts had long lines. The waterfall pool was crowded, and the lifeguards kept order, especially with the pre-teen boys who were running around like madmen. Salsa music seemed to surround the entire park.

"Okay, Gabby. Let's slow down a bit. It's time for your old abuelita to sit down and rest. Aren't you tired?"

"No, abuelita, I want to go back to the rides," Gabriella blurted.

"Okay, if it's all right with Ms. Panny, you two go. I will come in a few minutes, my love. I just have to take my shoes off for a bit," Olga begged.

"We will meet you near the big elephant, okay?" Gabriella said as she pulled on Theresa's arm. The two detectives followed Ms. Panny and Gabriella at a safe, twenty-yard distance.

When they got to the section of the park just before the rides, the scorching sun was suddenly covered by large, dark clouds as if it were about to rain.

"Gabriella, I think it may rain. It's best if we go back and collect abuelita, then make our way back to the car," Theresa offered.

"Aww, please, just one more ride," Gabriella pleaded.

Unexpectedly, a group of bikini-clad young women began dancing wildly in front of Theresa and Gabriella. The two detectives were enjoying the show of fake boobs and full, Dominican butts.

"Okay, Gabriella, that's our signal to go!" Theresa commanded.

Suddenly, a new, shiny, windowless, brown Ford panel van came rapidly onto the walkway between the tutor, her student, and their body-guards. Two stocky men with hoods covering their faces opened the sliding door of the vehicle. They snatched Gabriella and Theresa, pulling them roughly into the van. Theresa was seized around her waist and mouth, preventing her from screaming, by the taller of the two thugs. The other low-life simply grasped Gabriella off the ground like a sack of potatoes, leaving both of her sandals on the ground in front of the van. Gabriella let out a scream, "Miss Panny!" in the scant seconds it took for the ruffian to get her into the vehicle. The driver of the van took off speedily toward the park's exit.

By the time the two distracted detectives realized what had happened, it was too late. The van driver leaned on his horn, scattering the park's pedestrians in every direction. One of the detectives drew his firearm, to no avail. There were too many people in the park for the cop to fire, and his charges were already in the van.

Gabby and Theresa were gone.

# CHAPTER 44

"You mean to tell me these fuckers came into the park in a van and kidnapped the child and her teacher…right in front of you both?" Fumar hollered.

"General, sir…it happened in a flash. There was a lot of confusion in the park. We were standing there one second, and the next second they were gone," one of the detectives declared.

"Confusion?...Confusion? You fucking assholes! What kind of confusion could separate you from your assignment?" Fumar roared.

"There were a bunch of dancers…they…may have distracted us for a moment," the second detective blurted.

"You were looking at tits and ass instead of watching the child and her teacher, is that what you're telling me, you idiot?"

Both detectives looked down at their shoes in embarrassment. They knew full well their careers were ended.

Lieutenant Castillo entered the war room.

"General, the van was found on a side street in Bavaro, a few miles away from the park. It was stolen at the airport this morning. Also, regarding the dancing girls. They are locals who were at the waterslide pool. They had been given twenty dollars to dance at that location by a tall man with green eyes. Our men are getting their full statements.

"Any witnesses who can identify the assailants? Anyone see anything where the van was left?"

"Sir, one man was driving, and two men grabbed the girl and the teacher. They all wore woolen, commando-like masks. We are canvassing the street where the van was left for witnesses. So far, we have nothing. People are afraid to come forward. That area is a slum. No one sees or hears anything."

"Fumar? How in the fuck can my daughter and Theresa have been kidnapped in broad daylight with two of your men guarding them?" Vic blasted. He entered the room like a bull.

"Vic…I have no words for you," Fumar asserted.

"I have an hysterical wife upstairs. The doctor you sent for said Olga should be hospitalized. He gave her a sedative, but her heart is racing beyond…" Vic paused. He started to choke up.

"We will find your daughter, Vic, I swear this on my life. We are doing everything we can at the moment. In my experience, we need to wait for the kidnappers' demands. I know this will not bring you much comfort at the moment, but we have seen things like this before. It always ends with a payoff. These criminals are after money, nothing more."

"What a fucking country! Murdered prostitutes all over the place and kidnappings. Some fucking paradise this is," Vic screamed.

"Please try to stay calm. Let us do our job. Right now, we have to wait."

"Pardon me, General. Minister Castillo is on the phone," Lieutenant Castillo interrupted.

Fumar went to the telephone. Vic followed closely.

"Martinez, what the hell is going on there? My office received an anonymous call about the Gonnella girl being kidnapped. This is unacceptable to say the least, General."

"Sir, we are doing everything humanly possible to find the child and her teacher. There is no sense in me telling you the details. Suffice it to say, this was a professional job. The victims were taken in front of two of our officers."

"Two of our former officers, you mean. I want them arrested! I'm sending additional men from my office to Punta Cana. Colonel Ramirez will take over your duties on this and the serial killer case. You are finished!" Minister Castillo shrieked.

"Yes, sir," Fumar replied.

"Is Mr. Gonnella available?"

Fumar handed the phone to Vic.

"Minister?" Vic said.

"Mr. Gonnella, I offer you and your wife my sincerest of apologies. Know that we will do everything in our power to see your daughter is returned safely to you."

"That is all I want."

"I am replacing General Martinez today. You will soon meet his replacement, Colonel…"

"The fuck you will!" Vic hollered.

"Pardon me?"

"You heard me, Minister. The fuck you will replace the general at this juncture. I swear on my daughter, if you send one swinging dick here, I will personally break his fucking jaw."

"Mr. Gonnella, take hold of yourself!"

"Take hold of myself? You have no idea how in control of myself I am. I'm warning you, Minister. We are close to ending the case you hired us to solve. For all I know, my daughter's kidnappers are part of the case. Perhaps the killer set the whole thing up. General Martinez is staying with me all the way. Do you understand me?" Vic slammed the telephone down.

Vic turned to Fumar. "That fucker! That political hack! He's doing what's good for him, not for my daughter and Theresa. He wanted to replace you, now he sees an opportunity to get rid of you. Not happening. Better no one from Santo Domingo shows up here. I'll turn this place into a god damned battlefield."

Night followed day, and no contact was made from the kidnappers.

# CHAPTER 45

"This house is just amazing. I can't believe my eyes. I could get used to living here. With you especially," the chica cooed.

"You like it?"

"Are you joking? I don't think I've ever even seen a place this size. Not in Venezuela anyway, even when there was lots of money flying around. I never thought I would be inside a place that was so gorgeous. Thank you for bringing me to your home."

The two clicked glasses, then they shared a long, wet kiss.

"I'm amazed that when I kiss you, your braces don't get in the way."

"I've had plenty of practice with all the blow jobs I've given, I have to be a little careful. I never want to cut that thing." The girl winked at her host. They both laughed.

"Here, taste some delicious, fresh coconut. It's my favorite thing before a sex session."

"I love coconut. My father had three coconut trees on his property. That was before we lost everything. So sad."

The young brunette bit off some of the fruit, chewing it slowly, her red lips sensuously moving in a circular, teasing motion.

"I'm glad you like Brugal and not just beer like so many other girls from your country. There is something about a woman drinking beer from a bottle that is a turn off for me."

"Beer makes me full and uncomfortable, plus it tastes nasty. I love rum, but I think I can love you more."

"You're just saying that for a bigger tip. Don't worry, my love. You will be well taken care of."

"Brugal, that is pretty strong rum, my love. I feel a little light-headed, almost dizzy."

"It's working then."

"What? What do you mean? I...I feel...like I'm going to throw up or something."

"No throwing up in here, my dearest. I can't have that, you know. Here, let me put you out of your misery and choke you to death."

"What the fuck...what are you...?"

"Just let it go, my lovely whore. It will go much easier for you. Let the breath just seep out of you for the last time. I'm making you famous. Your name will soon be in all the newspapers. After all, you are being murdered by the famous Butcher of Punta Cana."

# CHAPTER 46

The sun rose at six-thirteen, promising a beautiful Punta Cana Saturday morning. Raquel and Vic tried to sleep near the phone in the war room to no avail.

Fumar and Lieutenant Castillo were already at the White House, pouring over maps of the area with six local policemen and several of his own men, trying fruitlessly to narrow down possibilities.

"I swear to you, Vic, if they harm my baby, I will hunt them down and kill them myself."

"Honey, they want money, that's all. They will release her as soon as they get what they want. These are professional kidnappers, just like Fumar said," Vic whispered. He was trying to comfort his woman, all the time his mind was racing with negative thoughts. He felt completely empty and useless. Vic's stomach was so tight, he thought of throwing up just to relieve the uneasy feeling of pressure.

"I blame myself. I never should have suggested she come along on this job. Gabby was safer at home. And then I never should have agreed to let her go to that fucking park," Raquel whimpered.

"Don't beat yourself up over these things. It's no one's fault. It was a great idea bringing her and your mom for a vacation. No one would have ever…"

"Do you think Ledon has anything to do with it? Do you think he's somehow figured out we are on his trail?"

"That occurred to me. He has the money and power to pull off a stunt like this. I'll deal with him, my way."

Suddenly, the door to the veranda swung open.

"Sorry to barge in, but your daughter means the world to me, too," John Deegan stated.

Fumar and his men rushed to apprehend the intruder.

"Hold up, Fumar! He's a friend of the family," Vic shouted.

"That's the first time you've referred to me as a friend. Not important at the moment. General, please join us, I have some information for all of you," Deegan announced.

Fumar took his unlit cigar from his mouth. The look on his face was nothing less than stupefied.

"May I ask who exactly you are, sir?"

"You heard the man. I'm a friend, a special friend. I'm working on getting the baby back home…TODAY! If my theory is correct, and my theories are generally spot on, you will all be amazed. I will add, I'm certain Gabby and her teacher are fine. However, before I leave you to determine if I truly am the genius people say I am, you need to hear what I found this morning."

"This morning? Found what?" Vic blurted.

"You asked me to check on the lawn at the Ledon Villa. I was to look for signs of dried blood in the soil and on the grass. Well, I snuck onto that property. I'm pretty good at being a sneak, you know. My government trained me well. I did as you asked and collected a few samples. The samples are unimportant at this point. Excuse me, can I have a cup of coffee...milk and sugar, please?" Deegan asked no one in particular.

"Coffee, you want a coffee?" Raquel screamed.

"Yes, milk and sugar, please."

One of the policemen ran to the coffee pot that Louisa had made in the kitchen.

"I can continue while my coffee is being made."

Fumar thought, This is a crazy man. The look on the general's face betrayed his thoughts.

"Yes, General, I am very eccentric. That comes with the territory of being on the edge of madness. Anyway, I believe there has been a fifth murder."

"What?" Vic shouted.

"Oh good, my coffee. Thank you, officer. Let me take a sip…ah perfect!"

"Jesus Christ almighty, John, get to the point," Raquel uttered.

"I took samples of the discolored grass, along with some soil. While doing that, I discovered some fresh blood on the grass, right where I found the stains during my first visit. The blood I found before dawn this morning, was still wet. Furthermore, there is residue of sand and gravel and a few wet tree leaves in the tires and on the floor of the fancy Ledon golf cart. I found some traces of blood on the back seat as well," Deegan pronounced.

"To my knowledge, there have been no reports of a body, sir," Fumar declared.

"Not yet. Go look near the beach. The gravel in the cart is similar to the gravel I've seen on roads here. Roads that are adjacent to the beach, near that La Cana golf course. That would account for the sand as well. Oh, and the leaves too. They are those skinny, green and yellow leaves I've seen on the trees near the ocean."

"General, I will take a few men and survey the area down by the beach between La Cana and the hotel," Castillo recommended. Fumar shook his head in approval. Castillo and three of the national police bolted toward the door. They took the four-person golf cart that was in the garage, as that area was merely a two-minute ride from the White House.

Fumar stood, towering over Deegan. "Sir, there is one major flaw in your theory regarding an alleged fifth murder. The flaw makes it difficult for me to take you seriously, if you will kindly forgive me."

"There is no alleged, General. There was a murder. Make book on that," Deegan remarked glibly.

"I spoke with my man in Cuba this morning. Mr. Ralph Ledon went to his room in Havana at three-thirty this morning. With two young prostitutes."

"Well perhaps they don't have enough blankets in his room," Deegan clowned.

"Ledon cannot have killed anyone in Punta Cana last night. Assuming there indeed was a murder committed. Ledon never left Havana."

"Did I ever say that Mr. Ledon was the murderer? Vic, Raquel, did you hear me say that? I don't recall saying that." Deegan pretended to be losing his memory.

"So, who is the Butcher of Punta Cana?" Raquel asked.

"I have my suspicions, but first we have to prove the murders, without any doubt, actually did take place at the Ledon villa. There could be several suspects. Perhaps the butler, anyone of the staff or workers, or simply a cunning someone who is using the villa to do their dirty work. Maybe someone with access to the home…the groundskeeper of the golf course also owns the company that does the Ledon landscaping, isn't that correct?"

Raquel interrupted Deegan, "Excuse me, you mean Freddy Reyes? We have had surveillance on him all day and night. I think we can eliminate him."

Vic stepped in, "Eliminate no one. Sorry to say, I have lost confidence in your department totally, General. You can take my remarks as personal if you want, but I don't think your men are all that swift. My daughter and her teacher were snatched up in broad daylight in front of your people. This man in front of you got into this villa just now, and he did it once before, posed as a gardener. Maybe Freddy Reyes somehow snuck out of his house or wherever he was. No…Freddy is still a suspect in my book, despite his living like a monk for a few days."

"You guys go and prove my theory. I'll get back to you on Gabby. You will get a call from the kidnappers soon, no doubt. See yas later," John said. His Bronx accent came through.

"Sir, I have one more silly question of you?" Fumar asked.

"Shoot!"

"How did you get past the guards in the back of this villa?"

"Good one, General. You see, I always have two cups of coffee in the morning…keeps me regular. I had the two coffees with me in nice paper cups with those nice plastic tops. I got them at the golf course this morning. They were actually free. When I walked up to the back of this house, I saw the two guards, gave them the coffee, thanked them for patrolling the villa, and told them I was Vic's father. I gotta go!"

# CHAPTER 47

"That friend of yours looks strangely familiar to me. I've seen his face somewhere, but I just can't recall where," Fumar declared.

Raquel glanced at Vic.

"Maybe he just has that kind of face," Vic blurted. "I must tell you, if anyone can help find my daughter, it's him."

"You called him John. What is his full name?" Fumar queried.

"Johnson…John Johnson. He's an old friend of the family, from New York," Vic lied.

"I see. At any rate, we still have to see if the old man is right. If another homicide pops up, we will have to…" Fumar was interrupted by his ringing cell phone. He looked at the caller I.D.

"Yes, Lieutenant."

"General, we found a body," Castillo stated.

"That fast? Hold on, I will put you on the speaker…go on, please," Fumar ordered.

"Yes, sir, just as that man advised, we found the body of a young woman. Looks like the fifth homicide by the same killer."

"Exactly where was she found?" Vic asked.

"Strangely, on a gravel and sand road between the La Cana golf course and condominium apartments, just before the Punta Cana Hotel property. Her body was just dropped in the brush along the road. Practically in plain view," Castillo responded.

"What was the condition of the body?" Fumar queried.

"She was naked, except for the burlap around her head. The body was cut, just as the others were. Her purse, with her identification and money, was left next to the body. It's as if the killer wants us to know who she was. The woman is a Venezuelan citizen who arrived in Punta Cana recently. Her passport was stamped last Monday. She was here only five days."

"Have you secured the area where she was found?" Fumar asked.

"Yes, sir. I can tell you that there are clear vehicle tracks that pulled up to the crime scene, turned around, and headed toward the exit to the compound. I've already sent detectives to see who entered and exited the gate. I have a feeling the killer did not use the gate, but knew the area and circumvented the security guards. We will soon find out what last night's security shift has to say."

"Well done, Castillo. Have you called the coroner?"

"Yes, of course, sir. He will be here at the scene any minute. He will take the body's temperature and be able to figure out an approximate time of death, but I believe her body is already in rigor mortis."

"Get back here as soon as you can, Lieutenant, I want to bring this Freddy in for questioning. We may be surprised at what we find," Fumar pronounced.

Theresa and Gabriella were unharmed, but frightened, in an old home owned by one of the kidnappers in the center of the worst neighborhood in Bavaro. Mangy, desperately thin, stray dogs walked up and down the road outside the ramshackle house, looking for any bits of food they could find. Old men drank beer and played dominos at a makeshift, tin shack bodega across the street, not knowing what was going on inside the kidnapper's lair.

"Make sure the girl and the woman don't see your faces. Everything is going perfectly according to my plan. You will be finished with your jobs soon," the leader of the kidnappers blurted.

"Should we feed them something?"

"No, a little hunger won't hurt them. They have plenty of water, that's all they need. I want you to call her parents in an hour at this number. Use the throw away cell I gave you. I'll be back at work by the time you call them. Ask for one million American dollars as we planned," the leader of the kidnappers ordered.

"And what about the pretty teacher?"

“That’s part of my plan. We release her first. In a gesture of good faith. I will then bring the girl to her parents, safe and sound. The money means nothing to me. I will pay all three of you as we agreed. Do exactly as I say. And Carlos, I see the way you behave around that teacher. Do not even think about touching her, or I will leave you where I find you, understood?”

The leader of the kidnapping crew left the dilapidated house and walked two blocks to an intersection crowded with Dominican prostitutes. Mopeds rushed around, zigging and zagging, rushing around in a frantic circus of humanity.

The leader jumped into the first taxi he saw.

“Take me near the airport. Do you know Tortuga Bay?”

“Yes, sir…very fancy,”

“Just drive quickly. I’ll tell you where to drop me off.”

The leader of the kidnappers wasn’t gone ten minutes before an argument ensued.

“Tell that kid to stop her whimpering!” Carlos, the kidnapper, demanded.

Gabriella was hugging Theresa and crying. The child was still upset after the trauma of being snatched at the park. She missed her mother and her daddy and abuelita and was tired and hungry. Theresa held Gabriella tightly to her chest and gently rocked her.

“My Spanish isn’t perfect, but you listen to me. She is a little girl, and little girls cry when they are upset. Don’t you have a sister or a daughter?” Theresa stated.

“Watch your mouth, sexy one, or I will give you something to cry about,” Carlos yelled. He grabbed his crotch and made a humping gesture.

“Carlos, leave her alone. We have a job to do,” the ruffian who drove the van blurted.

"I will do whatever I want. Maybe I want that big money instead of the bullshit pay he offered us. Besides, I want to show this American teacher what she has been missing all her life."

"Not while I'm here," the driver defied Carlos.

"I have a blade I will stick you with, faggot. Mind your own business."

"We made a deal. We keep to our word," the third kidnapper offered.

"We shall see. We shall see," Carlos uttered. His beady eyes glared at Theresa through his commando mask.

The driver took the highway toward the airport, practically not hitting his brake for the fifteen-minute ride to the airport. The kidnapper sat relaxed in the back seat of the taxi.

"At the circle, take the first exit."

"Yes, sir."

"Now drive straight until you see the Tortuga Bay sign. You will let me off there."

The kidnapper paid the driver his fare, then walked into the gated Tortuga Bay development toward the guard house.

A man was standing next to a late model car that seemed to have broken down. The hood of the vehicle was up, a red can of gasoline next to the rear of the car.

"Excuse me, young man. Would you kindly help me to start my car?"

"I have no time, old man,"

"You have no time to help someone in need?"

"Look, I told you I'm busy, wait for someone else to help you."

The older man suddenly rushed toward the kidnapper, shooting a stream of pepper spray directly into the abductor's face. The kidnapper dropped to his knees in severe pain, he could barely breathe and couldn't see at all. Unexpectedly, the old timer smashed the younger man on the side of his head with a small, black club, knocking him unconscious.

# CHAPTER 48

"Minister Castillo, there are developments you need to hear about. I appreciate you taking the time to get on this Skype call," Vic expressed.

"I see that Ms. Ruiz and General Martinez are in the room with you. First off, I am more concerned about having your daughter returned safely to you than this Butcher of Punta Cana case."

"With all due respect, Minister, that sounds nice and all, but I don't believe your words are sincere. Our daughter's kidnapping may very well be tied to the serial killer case, but we will soon know if that's true or not. Minister, you and I both know, once the word is leaked that a well-known American couple had their daughter kidnapped from right under the nose of your department, you can forget your beloved tourist trade from the States. This news will also destroy your department and your career, so stop the bullshit," Vic seethed.

"I am sorry you feel this way. Let's discuss the developments, please."

"Sure thing. We have found another murdered Venezuelan prostitute. That makes five in as many weeks. This killer is on a mission-oriented killing streak, which defies most modern intelligence on serial killer behavior. Believe me, Minister, he will not stop until he is captured or killed. The latest victim was found mutilated like the others and found basically in plain sight, so the perpetrator is more-or-less openly defying being apprehended. Most important for your knowledge and your knowledge only, we have reason to believe, at least this last homicide and possible others, were committed on the grounds of the Ledon villa," Vic paused. He was taking the minister's temperature.

"How is this even possible, Mr. Gonnella? Ledon is the pillar of our entire Dominican community," Minister Castillo replied.

"I understand about his money and influence…I get it, but you cannot block our investigation. If we have substantive and verified evidence that Ledon, or someone close to Ledon, is behind these homicides, we will need to interrogate him. Otherwise, any subsequent killings are on your head, Minister," Vic preached.

"General Martinez, are you in full agreement with the Gonnella assessment?"

"One hundred percent, Minister. Respectfully, sir, with your last order to me, you have tied my hands on this investigation. I will add that we are not saying Ledon is the killer. As a matter of fact, I have learned that he has an iron-clad alibi, unless he flew from Havana last night, came to Punta Cana to kill a woman, and then returned to Cuba."

"Or has the gift of bi-location," Raquel added.

"Like Jesus Christ, Ms. Ruiz," Castillo uttered.

"Yes, like Jesus, and a few others."

"General, I hear your frustration. I would like to bring this matter to the attention of President Medina himself. I have to answer to him on this sensitive Ledon matter. I will contact you with a decision within the hour."

"One more thing, Minister. Our guests have received a call from the kidnappers. They are demanding a ransom, as we expected," Fumar announced.

"What are their terms, General?"

"One million American dollars. Not our pesos. They made that very clear. The funds are to be delivered by Ms. Ruiz to a place yet to be determined, at which time the child and her teacher will be released."

"I will arrange for the funds to be sent to you in Punta Cana, General."

"I've already made those arrangements, Minister. My Sicilian grandfather told me, 'nothing scratches your skin like your own fingernails,' and I intend to follow his advice," Vic stated.

🗡 🗡 🗡

"After I shot that crap into your face and bashed you nicely in your coco, I gave you a little something to calm you down and let you sleep a while," Deegan offered. He was speaking to the kidnapper.

"Who are you? Where is this place?"

"Not far from where I met you. I was waiting for you to return today because I figured out your sick game. They tell me I'm a genius, ya know." The kidnapper was tightly bound to a large oak tree around the waist and shoulders by a yellow, nylon rope, the kind sold in hardware stores. His legs were splayed out in front of him. Both legs were tied down with the same rope and bolted into the ground with steel posts. The man's slacks were sliced from the hem up to his crotch.

"Who are you? What do you want from me?"

"I was considered the foremost serial killer since John Wayne Gacey. Except I didn't hurt children. Only real bad guys. Guys like you. Maybe. None of my victims died easily, there was always a lot of blood and a lot of pain…you see, I know how to kill. I was trained to do that by my country… kill. I can do it fast or slowly, depending on my mood or the infraction of the person I am killing. Here, let me show you who I am on my cell phone. I can Google my name, and maybe then, you will understand your fate. Google is a sort of résumé on my deeds."

Deegan open a Google link to his crimes. "Here is a good one, brings back memories," Deegan laughed.

Lopez looked at the phone that Deegan held up to his face. An article from the New York Times with the headline, "SERIAL KILLER ESCAPES IN ROME, ITALY," complete with a full- face photo of John Deegan.

"This can't be! How am I here with you? Oh, my God!" Lopez shrieked.

Deegan held the photo up to his face. "See? Do I look like I aged any?"

"Are you crazy, old man? Do you know who I am?"

"Some would say I'm crazy. I don't think so, but…anyway, to answer your question, I know very well who you are. My question is, do YOU know who you are?" Deegan asked.

"What? Do I know who I am? Of course I do!" the kidnapper shouted.

"Shouting won't help. We are far enough into the bush that only the birds can hear you. Frankly, it would take anyone months, perhaps years, to find your putrid bones."

"Why pick me for your silly game?"

"Game? Yes, it is a game to me. Seriously speaking, life is a game to me. Xs and Os, stickball, potsey, tag, skully, games I played as a kid, but I figured out how to win all the time. But, I digress. I picked you because you took someone I care about. My darling Gabriella."

"I don't know what you're talking about, old man. You better just let me go and walk away. Do you know I'm a policeman?"

"Oh yes, I do! You are Sergeant Manuel Castillo of the Ministry of the Interior and Police."

"It would be wise if you released me."

"It would be wiser if you told me where Gabriella and her teacher are being held."

"No idea what you are talking about, you old fool."

"I see that you need to be convinced, but first let's discuss how I figured things out about you. Let's see...Your daddy is a big shot who kisses ass in Santo Domingo so well that you will be made a colonel in the police department before you're forty. But that isn't good enough for you, because you are a spoiled little fuck. So, you step on people, use people, destroy people along the way. Now you have a thing for that pretty teacher...I get that, I was young once...all that testosterone. But you want what you want, when you want it. With me so far, Manny?"

"Fuck you!"

"I don't want to get too far off track. So now you get the bright idea to make yourself look good to your country and to the pretty American girl. You have the child kidnapped for a variety of reasons, but mostly because you want to be the hero, bringing the little girl back to her family. Your father would be proud, President Medina will give you an award. Your promotion to whatever you want, let's say Captain, is done overnight, and you are on your way to the top. Maybe even a political career. Why not? After all, you are a big hero." Deegan stopped speaking and walked around the tree out of Lopez's view.

"That must be scary! All tied up with a maniacal old fart going behind you. I just went there to retrieve an implement. It's now in my belt under this nice Tommy Bahama shirt. I like Tommy Bahama shirts...very thinning, don't you think?"

Lopez's eyes were practically bulging out of their sockets, his shirt and the back of his pants were stuck to his body from his profuse perspiration. Mosquitos were swarming on his forehead and neck.

"Here is the deal I'll make with you. I like deals. You can actually get away with this, well somewhat, anyway. One time offer. Take it or die."

"I'm listening," Lopez blurted. He was moving his head around, trying to stop the bugs from biting his unprotected skin.

"You tell me where the girl and the teacher are. I get them. I come back and release you. I tell no one about your involvement, so you get to avoid prison and a destroyed reputation for your family. Here is the catch. You leave the Dominican Republic, never to return. Well, you can actually return after my death. If you come back here while I'm alive, I'll know about it and get back here and slaughter you like a pig. Literally like a pig."

"How will I know if you will return after you get the girl?"

"You don't."

"I don't think so. What is my percentage that I'll even live a few days here?"

"On the other hand, I can force you to tell me what I want to know. And then bleed you out right here."

Lopez hung his head and didn't reply.

"Okay, light is burning. Here we go!" From his waistband behind his back, Deegan exposed an unopened, all-silver, eight-inch switchblade knife. He snapped the blade open. It was long, thin, and deadly sharp.

Deegan ran the knife slowly under Lopez's nose, just enough for the captured man to feel the coolness of the blade.

"I used to use wood to kill my victims. I'm sure you've heard of me. I'm John Deegan, the guy who slaughtered all those fuckers, who harmed kids. Ya know, priests, rabbis, coaches, teachers, like that."

Lopez's eyes widened. He knew of the Deegan case and how Vic Gonnella and Raquel Ruiz became famous. Lopez had researched Gonnella when he learned they were coming to search for the Butcher of Punta Cana.

"Mother of Jesus!" Lopez screamed.

"Just because you may change your mind and give me the place where you have the girl, I'll start carving you from the legs and crotch. I was known for the jugular vein, for expediency, mind you. Yes, I realize it's a mess, squirting blood all over the fucking place, but the bugs will appreciate the meal."

Deegan ran the tip of the knife on the inside of Lopez's leg, from his ankle to just under his testicles, leaving a thin, bloody slice that resembled a crooked river on a map.

Lopez sucked in air through his teeth as he tried to deal with the pain. He finally surrendered his will with a scream that sounded like a cross between a rhesus monkey and an eleven-year-old girl.

"I have so much experience with giving pain, it becomes another game to me. You must decide if you will give me the address I want or die slowly from excruciating pain and blood loss. Believe me when I tell you, I can keep you alive for a long time, Manny dear."

"If I die, you will never find the girl!" Lopez shouted.

"Oh, I'll find her because I'll figure your posse out. And I'll kill them where I find them. But you will be dead, and your body will be picked at by bugs and small rodents. Lovely!"

"Please, I meant that girl no harm. I planned to return her, not even take the money. It's true what you said. I wanted to be thought of as a hero cop who risked his neck to save a kidnapped little girl and her teacher."

"I'm so glad you have confessed, Manny. You may even get a ticket to heaven with that line of crap you're spewing. Deegan took a nice slice out of the sergeant's left ear lobe. Lopez's screech, send birds flying from the trees in every direction.

"You sick fuck!" Lopez whimpered.

"We can discuss my last psychological evaluation in a moment. But first, I have an important decision to make. Perhaps you can help me choose?"

"Choose? Choose what?" Lopez blubbered.

"I'm trying to decide if I should take the tip of your nose or the tip of your dick?"

"No...no... please...enough! I've had enough."

"You owe me an address, my dear Manny. And make no mistake, if I go to the address you provide and the girl is not there, I will be very pissed off when I return. Trust me on this, you will call for your mama and plead for death," Deegan whispered.

"They are in a small house, about three miles from the park where she was taken. It's on Villa Espinosa, number 8."

"How many of your people are there? And please don't lie to me. That makes me crazy when someone lies to me."

"Three, only three. I swear on everything I love."

# CHAPTER 49

Jimmy and Jack secured the one million dollars in cash through Vic's contacts at Citibank, Banco Popular, and two other banks that were able to help with the large amount of cash needed for the ransom.

"Now we wait for instructions," Fumar stated.

"Listen to me, Fumar. I do not want any heroics. When I get my daughter and Theresa back safely, they can keep the fucking money. Is that clear?" Vic demanded.

"We will make no moves to retrieve your money. Once they are safe, then it's in my hands."

"Agreed."

Raquel walked into the room after she had left for a few minutes. "My mother is having another episode with her heart. Vic, this whole mess is just too much for her. The doctor gave her another sedative. I think we need to send her back to New York now. I'm afraid we're going to lose her," Raquel lamented.

Raquel was totally exhausted from lack of sleep and an abundance of worry, but she had no intention of leaving the Dominican Republic without her child.

"Air Ambulance is ready to go at Punta Cana International. I chartered their jet. They will take her to any hospital we want. They have a registered nurse to accompany your mother and plenty of equipment on board if needed, honey. They can land at any New York area airport," Vic answered.

"Her cardiologist is at Hackensack Medical Center. You know how mama is. She insists on going to Jersey to see him."

"It's five minutes from Teterboro. That's it, then!" Vic commanded.

"Vic, Raquel, we will do whatever is needed for your mother, but I think the medical care is much better back home," Fumar declared. The general continued, "There is another development you need to hear."

"About Gabby?" Raquel screamed.

"No...no, I'm sorry. My man in Havana just informed me that Ledon just boarded his jet to Punta Cana. He will be back here in less than two hours," Fumar reported.

"I'll meet that prick at the airport," Vic shouted.

"Vic, I'm pleading with you. Now is not the time for any craziness. We have plenty of time to get Ledon. On our terms, please," Fumar begged.

"Fumar is right, honey, let's not telegraph our move," Raquel added.

Lieutenant Castillo broke in. "General, Ralph Ledon is on the telephone. He wants to speak with Mr. Gonnella."

"Get the fuck out of here!" Vic uttered. "The balls on this guy!"

"Take the call, Vic. And above all, stay calm. Don't get your Sicilian temper in this," Raquel advised.

Vic went to the phone. He composed himself with a deep breath.

"Gonnella."

"Mr. Gonnella, this is Ralph Ledon. I'm calling you from the air. I will be in Punta Cana shortly. I've been informed of this terrible situation with your daughter and her tutor. I called to tell you that I am at your service to help you in any way possible. In spite of our disagreement, this is still your baby. Nothing is more important than her safe return."

Vic was stunned speechless.

"Mr. Gonnella, are you there...hello?"

"Yes, I'm here. I'm overwhelmed by your call." Vic's mind was racing.

"Pay these men whatever they are asking. I will give you the money. Let's get your daughter back."

"Thank you. We have what we need, but your generosity is..."

"May I come to your villa and offer my personal assistance? I have a big reach, as you will see."

"Ahh...Yes, please, you are welcome here. I can't thank you enough."

"See you soon!"

Vic looked at the phone after Ledon disconnected.

"This guy is good. He is very good. Maybe he is using Gabby's kidnapping to mask his crimes, or maybe he is behind the kidnapping to cover for someone else," Vic articulated.

"Or maybe he is sincere and really wants to help us?" Raquel added.

"I still say he was not anywhere near Punta Cana when the last girl was murdered," Fumar said.

"We will see. I just don't trust the motherfucker," Vic seethed.

# CHAPTER 50

Deegan drove like the wind in his rented car back to Bavaro. He used Google Maps to find the house at Espinoza. He wore the same farmer clothing and straw hat he used when he walked up on Vic and Raquel in the backyard of the White House.

He parked the car a few blocks away from the decrepit house where Lopez confessed that Gabriella, Theresa, and his three confederates were held up. Deegan walked like the old man he often portrayed.

*I'm pretending to be an old man, but damn it, I am an old man,* Deegan thought.

Deegan looked over at the house where Gabriella and Theresa were being held captive. He turned his attention to his intermediate target.

"Hola, can I join you men in a game of dominos?" Deegan asked.

No reply came from the old men sitting around the bodega across the street from number 8. The group was not used to strangers.

"I will buy the Presidente for everyone," Deegan announced.

Three of the old codgers slowly stood, one of them moved the domino board onto an old, beat-up, pink, plastic table. John was offered a red, plastic milk crate as a seat.

"When a man offers us beer, we play. My name in Luis, this is Papo, and this good-looking guy over here is Pedro," Luis declared. All three men looked to be in their eighties. In fact, the oldest one was only sixty-six, a testament to their difficult lives.

"I am Juan, my friends call me Juanito," John said. The bodega owner served four, ice-cold bottles of Presidente beer.

"I like to call you flaco," Luis laughed.

"I haven't been called flaco before, so you can call me that," Deegan laughed, patting his slim stomach. Deegan was now thinner than he ever was in his entire life. Beating cancer had taken its toll.

Papo mixed the domino tiles in a rapid, circular motion, like he did it a million times before.

Everyone drew their seven dominoes. Deegan drew the double six. Pedro, sitting across from Deegan, started the game. After the first twelve minutes, Luis and Papo beat Pedro and Deegan by forty-seven points. Papo slammed his winning domino onto the table for the dramatic win.

"Sorry, Pedro, I'm a little rusty," Deegan blurted. The three Dominicans laughed aloud, and everyone took a long pull on the bottled beer.

As Pedro, the loser, shuffled the ivory white tiles for the second game, Deegan, his eye on the house across the street, ordered a second round of beer.

"I'm thinking about getting a room nearby. Does anyone know if a cheap room or house is available?" Deegan asked.

"My sister-in-law rents a room down the street. There is only one problem," Luis stated.

"What kind of problem?" Deegan queried.

"In the night, she will scratch on your door."

Deegan looked perplexed.

"She is called con culo. She will sit on top of you with her big ass," Luis revealed. Everyone laughed heartily.

"What about that house across the street? It looks empty," Deegan noted.

"Someone lives there. He's a real troublemaker. Stay away, my friend," Luis stated. He waved his finger back and forth to support his negative opinion.

The dominos game came to its two-hundred-point end within thirty-five minutes. Deegan and Pedro lost embarrassingly.

"One more round for you nice men. I hope to practice and play with you again."

Deegan shook each man's hand, paid the bodega owner in pesos for the beers, and slowly walked up the street.

He walked around the street to the rear of the troublemaker's house. Deegan made his way through another tumbledown edifice, through a gray, cinder block-littered backyard.

Deegan cautiously peered inside the house. He could see Theresa and the sleeping, shoeless Gabriella, but none of their captors were in sight.

Scratching at the back door as a cat or dog would, Deegan stood aside the door and waited. He scratched again, a bit louder.

"Go see what that is," Carlos commanded.

The driver of the van walked to the peeling, paint-starved, wooden door, looked out the door's window, and saw nothing. Deegan reached his hand around, scratching low at the door.

The hapless criminal pulled open the door, saw nothing, and stepped out into the decrepit yard for further investigation.

Deegan sprung on him, pulling the criminal by his arm onto the ground. With practiced precision, Deegan slit the driver's throat, severing his jugular vein in a spray of blood. The ill-fated abductor was dead before he even knew what had happened.

Looking into the house, Deegan made his way to Theresa. She was nodding out on a mattress next to the sleeping child. Gently, Deegan put his hand over the teacher's mouth, startling her.

"Stay very quiet, young lady. I'm here to help you. I'll be a few minutes. Don't stir Gabriella."

Theresa, wide eyed, frantically nodded her head.

Deegan moved stealthily toward the next room. Long, multi-colored beads on the door separated the two rooms.

Carlos was playing a game on his cell phone, the third gangster was asleep on a ragged sofa.

Deegan moved quickly through the beads. Carlos tried to jump to his feet, panicked by the intruder. Deegan stuck the long, thin knife he had used on Manny Lopez into the thug at the base of the back of his skull. He could feel the man's body trembling through the blade. Carlos' spinal cord severed, and he fell dead into a heap onto the bare, wooden floor.

Deegan slowly wiped the blade on the dead man's shirt. The third goon never stirred. Deegan moved deliberately toward the chair and the unfortunate, sleeping criminal.

"Coño, rise and shine, sleeping beauty," Deegan whispered into the man's ear.

The startled fool tried to focus his sleepy eyes to no avail. Deegan took the same knife he used on Carlos, tearing out the man's larynx in a circular, almost surgical, movement.

"The Butcher of Punta Cana indeed," Deegan whispered.

# CHAPTER 51

"Hi, daddy!"

"Gabriella? Baby! Oh my God! Where are you?" Vic exploded.

"I'm in a car with Miss Panny. We are coming home.

"What car? Whose car?"

"Your friend, John. Here hold on, he wants to talk to you."

"Vic, all is well. She is unharmed, as is Theresa," Deegan announced.

Raquel could hear her daughter's voice on Vic's cell. "Is she ok?" Raquel blurted.

Vic nodded and smiled, giving the thumbs up sign. Raquel made the sign of the cross, then broke into a happy sob.

"Jesus Christ, how? How did you find her? Where was she?" Vic asked. The constant pit in his stomach vanished as quickly as when he first got it.

"That's a story for another day. I did have to break a promise I made, though," Deegan added.

"Promise? What promise?"

"You have so many questions, Gonnella. We will be back within the next twenty minutes or so, then I have to run out and tend to some unfinished business."

"Oh my God! I…I don't know what to say!"

"Just tell your cook to make some chicken fingers or whatever kids eat these days. Gabby is famished. Get some ice cream, too. Ice cream is comfort food, ya know. Theresa says hi."

Vic could hear his daughter clapping and saying yay in the background. Deegan ended the call as Deegan always does.

"She's safe. John has them both. They are on their way back," Vic announced.

Raquel jumped into her man's arms, crying tears of joy into his shoulder.

"How did he find her? How did he get her back?"

"I have no clue at the moment, but in typical fashion, he said he had to break a promise. I have no idea what he means."

"A promise? I can't even think right now. Let's go tell mama," Raquel blurted.

The couple ran up the stairs, taking two steps at a time to Olga's bedroom suite.

Louisa was sitting in a chair next to Olga's bed, holding the stricken abuelita's hand.

"Mama, we found Gabriella! She's on her way back here. She's fine," Raquel announced.

"I know!" Olga stated. She looked so much better than just a few hours ago.

"You know? How do you know?"

"This morning, Tia Carmen came to me in a dream. She said the baby would be fine and would be home today. She has never disappointed me. Now, I have to get up, and get ready to greet my granddaughter. I need to dress and put on some makeup. The way I look now will only scare my darling Gabby."

Fumar and Lieutenant Castillo remained down in the war room.

"I am not calling your uncle until that child is in her mother's arms," Fumar stated.

"General, please, I am not being disrespectful to your office, but please don't refer to the minister as my uncle. He is an uncle only by blood," Castillo declared.

"I apologize, Lieutenant. It won't happen again."

Raquel stayed with her mother, helping her to get out of bed and dressed.

Vic was halfway down when Castillo came running up the staircase.

"Mr. Gonnella, Ralph Ledon has arrived."

This will be interesting, Vic thought.

"Mr. Gonnella. I wish I were seeing you under better circumstances," Ledon articulated.

"Thank you for coming, Mr. Ledon, I greatly appreciate your concern."

"It is the very least I can do. Have you heard any more from the kidnappers?"

"No, we are still awaiting instructions," Vic lied.

Fumar spoke up, "I have told Mr. Gonnella and Ms. Ruiz that we are dealing with professional criminals who only seek a big payday. However, every precaution must be taken," Fumar pronounced. The general followed Vic's lead, not letting Ledon in on the call they just received.

"Do you have the funds in place, General?" Ledon queried.

Vic answered, "We are all set, but thank you for your generous offer."

"Is there anything I can do for you at this moment?"

"No, Mr. Ledon, I can't think of anything we need right now, but I will call you if we need any help," Vic answered.

Batista, the house boy, brought out a tray of coffee for the men. They sat and sipped the hot coffee while discussing the abduction.

After a few minutes, the honking of a car's horn could be heard from outside the house. It reminded Vic of when a bride and groom were leaving the church. Loud, rapid beep-beeps in no order. The sound of the policemen clapping and cheering was muffled until Batista opened the villa's front door.

"She's here! They are both here! Thanks to Jesus!" Batista praised.

The sound of Raquel's voice coming down the stairs screaming, "My baby" brought Fumar and Castillo to tears.

Vic raced to the car, lifting his Gabriella out of the back seat into his arms. Theresa exited the back seat, wiping away tears of joy, as she made her way to Vic and his daughter. Raquel rushed to embrace her daughter and Vic, with kisses and hugs flying around each other's faces.

Fumar, Castillo, and Ralph Ledon were smiling and clapping from the doorway. Ledon, taken by the emotion and love in the scene of a family being united, was brought to tears as well. Olga made her way slowly past the men in the doorway. She stood there with her open arms reaching to the sky. Her lips were moving as though she was talking to the heavens. At the sight of her grandmother, Gabriella began to sob deeply.

In all of the happy pandemonium, John Deegan slowly drove out of the driveway and away from the villa.

# CHAPTER 52

Deegan drove his rental back to the spot in the deep forest brush where he had left Sergeant Manuel Lopez.

"Jesus Christ on the cross, the bugs are eating me alive. Please, I'm begging you to release me. I swear I will disappear. No one will ever see me in this country ever again, please."

Lopez's legs were caked in his own dried blood. Flies and engorged mosquitoes were feasting the length of his leg. His head, face, and neck were inflamed by massive bites. His feet were swollen from the poison infused into his body.

Deegan wore a Cheshire grin on his face.

"How do you like my outfit, Manny? I think it makes me look like a real old, Dominican worker. And I look even skinnier than I do in my regular street clothes. Actually, the guys at the bodega, across from the address you gave me, called me flaco. They were totally fooled. They certainly knew I wasn't Dominican by my Spanish. Actually, I sound like I'm from Nicaragua, don't you think? At any rate, you didn't lie, so now I have to decide what to do with you, Sergeant."

"But...I thought we had a deal! I gave you the girl, and you..."

"Yeah, yeah, I know. But, here is my dilemma on that deal. I've been in hiding for a very long time. Living nicely, quietly minding my own business, and I find myself in Punta Cana to help old friends. Then I tell you who I am. Then...well then, I get you to roll over on your crew. So now, if I let you live, to save your fucking bitch ass as they say, you will tell everyone the infamous John Deegan was the guy who killed three vermin in that house in Bavaro. Next thing I know, they will call me, among many other things, the Butcher of Punta Cana. Everyone will think I killed those poor girls. All of a sudden, everyone is after me again, to stick me inside a prison for the time I have left. What would you do if you were me, Manny?"

"I swear on my soul, I will leave this country, I will never mention your name. Never!"

"You swear on your soul, yet you really have no soul, Sergeant Lopez. And if I was tied to that tree, you would either shoot me or leave me to die slowly. Oh, by the way, I have your gun. I took it off your ankle when I bashed your head. I can shoot you, leave you here to die from thirst or exposure or maybe small animals that will pick at you. You know, wild dogs have been known to be able to smell blood from a good distance."

"Please, I know I was greedy. I know I was seeking fame. I did the wrong thing. I am begging you to forgive me."

"On the other hand, I let you go, and then what? You go hide out for a while with daddy's money, and things ain't so bad for you. Then you find out that I croak, and you come back home, nobody knows you kidnapped the girl and her teacher, and you pick up where you left off. Is that a good deal for me?"

Lopez began to sob like a child. He saw his death was coming.

"On the other hand, I've heard people say forgiveness is divine. What do you think, Manny?"

"Yes! Yes...God will forgive you for anything you've done."

"That's another problem for me, Manny pal. I don't think I believe in that kind of God. I did at one time, but I'm not sure anymore."

🗡 🗡 🗡

"Captain Gebhardt, please prepare my jet to return to Lugano-Agno airport. I miss my home and my wife. How is the weather in Switzerland?"

"Clear skies, sir."

"Okay, home then."

"Yes, sir, what time would you like to leave?"

"Let me see. I'm thirty minutes from Aeroporto Punta Cana. I have to return the rent-a-car. Let's say an hour," Deegan replied.

"Yes, sir. I will prepare my flight plan."

# CHAPTER 53

"You were one of the first on the scene where the body was found after Tony, the caddie, called it in, is that correct, Mr. Reyes?" Vic asked through an interpreter.

"Yes, I was. The call came from the caddie master. I happened to be with the general manager in his office in the pro shop," Freddy answered.

Vic, Fumar, and Lieutenant Castillo were interviewing Freddy Reyes in a conference room at Punta Espada.

Freddy continued, "This is kind of embarrassing for me. You guys come to my place of work and basically drag me into this room. The whole place is wondering what's going on."

"Would you rather we have called you into police headquarters and treated you like a criminal? We asked to see you like gentlemen, and we are behaving as such," Fumar answered. The general's cold stare turned Freddy's blood cold. Freddy decided not to complain any more.

Vic continued, "I want to know your opinion on how the girl's body got to the coral cave on your course."

"My opinion? Well, if I were to guess, she was either carried or was driven to that spot. For all I know, she was murdered there," Freddy responded.

"The evidence shows she was murdered not far from Punta Espada. Our forensics further indicate that she was driven there in a golf cart or similar vehicle. Perhaps it was one of the vehicles that your people use to maintain the course," Castillo added.

"We have many vehicles which are used on this course. I have no idea how she was brought there. I'm not a detective," Freddy said. His tone bordered on sarcastic.

"Do you have any workers that you would consider to be someone who could have done this homicide?" Vic asked.

"I have twelve men working on the course in two shifts. Feel free to interview them. I can't think of any of my men who are capable of doing this. They are all hard workers with families. Been with me for years."

"Do all twelve have access to all the vehicles and golf carts?" Castillo queried.

"The maintenance vehicles, yes, they do. The carts are locked up after the last golfers are finished. At sundown, the golf carts are all locked up in what we call the barn."

"Where is this barn?" Castillo followed.

"Right below this building."

"We will be bringing in all of the twelve men of yours for questioning. Perhaps we can find something from them. Perhaps they saw something," Fumar added.

"Do you have any security on the course at night?" Castillo inquired.

"Yes, only one guard, but he is stationed at the club house until dawn. He doesn't go out on the course."

"So, no one would see you if someone went out late at night with a chica, correct?" Vic asked.

"What? What are you talking about, sir?"

"What we are talking about, Mr. Reyes, is a report we have from a Venezuelan woman who claims you took her out to the sea, late at night, and left her there," Castillo blurted.

Freddy looked like a deer caught in a car's headlights. He shifted uneasily in his chair. Beads of sweat began to form on his forehead.

"Me? What woman? I don't understand."

"A woman who claimed you used her services on several occasions," Fumar stated.

Freddy pretended to search his memory.

"You don't think I had anything to do with this killing, do you?"

"Just answer our questions, Mr. Reyes. If I think for one second you are telling us some bullshit, I will drag your skinny ass down to headquarters, and then I will not behave like a gentleman," Fumar added. Although there was a no smoking sign, Fumar lit a long Churchill on which he had been chewing.

"Okay, yes, there was a woman I brought out one night some time ago. Yes, she was a chica."

"A Venezuelan?" Castillo asked.

"Yes."

"And your purpose to bring her out on the course late at night?" Vic asked.

Freddy felt bombarded by all three men. He began to perspire heavily. His forehead was soaked, as was his shirt.

"My purpose? Honestly, to have sex. That's all. Is that illegal?"

"And you left her out near the water on the coral, after threatening to throw her into the sea on a pitch-black night?" Vic inquired.

"I wanted to scare her. That's all!" Reyes shouted.

"Why would you do such a thing? Why would you threaten to kill her?" Vic followed.

"Look, she was a chica, and yes, I paid her several times. The puta fell in love with me. She was calling me all the time. She even showed up at my apartment. She wanted me to take her in so she could marry me and get a visa."

"She asked you to marry her?" Castillo asked.

"More than once, yes, she did."

"So, you brought her out on the course, late at night, had sex with her in the vehicle, then said you would throw her in the ocean, and left her there, is that correct?"

"Yes. I wanted to get rid of her. I don't need that shit in my life."

"How did you get the cart if they are locked up all night, Mr. Reyes?" Castillo queried.

"Sir, I am the groundskeeper. I have all the keys to the place."

"Did she contact you after that evening?" Fumar asked.

"No, sir, never!" Freddy replied.

"So, your little drama worked, didn't it?" Castillo blurted.

"Evidently, yes. But I will say, I never did that again, and I never hurt any chica."

"How did you meet this Venezuelan?" Vic asked.

"Through someone I know. I got other chicas from him."

"Who is that someone, Reyes?" Fumar questioned.

"Do I have to say a name? I'm not one to…"

"Answer the fucking question!" Fumar hollered.

"It was…a guy named Lenny."

"Lenny? Just Lenny. I bet there are ten Lennys in Punta Cana," Fumar seethed.

"Lenny Diaz. He's a pimp. He hangs around Mi Casa Lounge."

"Did this Lenny provide you with drugs? Marijuana, cocaine?"

"I don't do drugs, sir. Never have."

"Your answers are noted. Keep in mind, this is an open investigation, Reyes. You are free to go now; however, you are to surrender your passport, pending further questioning. Officers will accompany you to your home. While they are there to retrieve your passport, they will look through your home for other evidence," Fumar stated.

"Will the general manager know of this? I mean, will he know I took the chica out on the course?"

"I see no reason why we should tell him. Unless, of course, there is other evidence we find," Fumar offered.

"I appreciate that, sir. I wouldn't want to lose my job here."

"One more thing, Mr. Reyes," Vic said. "Do you have access to burlap?"

"Burlap? Wait a minute, because the girl who was found in the cave had burlap on her head?

"Mr. Reyes, just answer my question. Do you have any access to burlap?"

"Yes, sir, I do. But I never killed anyone!"

"What do you use burlap for, and where do you get it?"

"It comes in on the bottom of some trees that are planted here and there on the course. Mostly, we bury the trees with the burlap still attached. If we peel the burlap off the trees, we discard it."

"Have a nice rest of your day, Reyes. Don't leave Punta Cana without my approval," Fumar commanded.

"I don't believe Reyes is a suspect," Vic said. The three men were in Fumar's car.

Fumar relit his Churchill. "I agree. If he is telling us the truth, and he wanted to chase that chica away, he decided to terrify her. Let's put our attention on the Ledon Villa."

# CHAPTER 54

When Vic returned to the White House, he went right to see Gabriella and Theresa. Raquel and their daughter were taking a much-needed nap together. Tears came to Vic's eyes, seeing the two of them curled up together. That could have turned out not so well. *Maybe I need to go back to church,* Vic thought. The momentary idea of returning to his church put a shiver up Vic's spine.

"I need to call Deegan. He's been awfully quiet," Vic said in a whisper.

"Hello, Deegan."

"Hello, Gonnella," Deegan sounded a bit tired.

"You okay?"

"Never better. I'm sitting with Gjuliana at the moment. We are looking at the most beautiful moon you've ever seen. It's lighting up the whole sky and casting its lovely beam onto Lake Lugano."

"What? Areyoukiddinmeorwhat?" Vic's Bronx came roaring out. "You're in fucking Switzerland?"

"No, just Switzerland," Deegan replied.

Vic fumbled for what to say next. "You…you left Punta Cana without saying goodbye? Without us thanking you for saving Gabriella?"

"Now you and I both know I had to high-tail it out of there. That General kept looking at me in the car like he was trying to figure me out. I think he recognized me but couldn't put his long fingers on it."

"Deegan! C'mon, that's bullshit. If he had made you, he would have said something."

"Wrong again, Gonnella. Just when I think I've taught you enough, you go off the rails on me. It won't be long until that General figures out I was there. Did you forget I'm still an international fugitive? I have a pretty good bounty still on my noggin."

"Cut it out, will ya please? If Fumar had made you, he would have said something."

"You are being silly now," Deegan chuckled.

"You left yesterday?"

"I did indeed. I broke my promise to you, and I had to skedaddle for my own good."

"I still can't figure that out. What promise do you mean?"

"You said way back when, if I ever killed anyone again, you would hunt me down and kill me yourself. I couldn't take that chance."

"Like I would really do that? I figured you out already. The police got an anonymous call about three bodies that were found in a piece-of-shit hut in Bavaro. Fumar and Castillo want to talk with Theresa, ya know, show her some photos to identify those knuckleheads as the kidnappers. She's still shaken up, so we asked for a couple days. From what I heard how they died, it was your signature all over the place. Three for the good-guys is how I see it."

"Four!"

"What? Four?"

"Sergeant Lopez. I had to introduce him to his Lord and Savior."

"What? Why the fuck?"

"He masterminded the kidnapping of my dear Gabriella and Theresa. He wanted to be the one who seemingly saved them and returned them safely and unharmed. He admitted even more to me at the end, I offered him a sort of last confession so he could get into heaven. He admitted that he planned to shoot all three of the men I iced. I think he saw himself as being heralded as a national hero. He's gone now. His body may be found at some point."

"I'll be dipped in shit!" Vic shouted.

"And now I know you will come to kill me. I'm ready to go, Gonnella," Deegan said with a laugh.

"I'll come for you all right, Deegan. I'll come to kiss you on that noggin of yours."

"Vic, I'm getting old. The fast ball is gone. I still can throw the curve now and again, but the heat is gone. I'm running out of time, Gonnella. I'm not sure if we will ever see each other again. Go marry that woman, and kiss that baby for me."

Deegan hung up as he was known to do.

# CHAPTER 55

Olga bounced back from the abyss once Deegan returned Gabriella safe and sound to the child's family.

"Mama, I was so worried about you. I was so afraid of losing you. Our lives would be so different, so empty, if you weren't here with us. I don't mean here in Punta Cana, I mean here with us as a family," Raquel lamented.

"My sweet daughter, the time will come when the Lord calls me, and you will understand the cycle of life. That's why I almost gave up on living. If anything had happened to Gabby, I would have preferred to be dead than to keep living. A parent should never see their child go before them. I guess I'm too old to face that kind of tragedy. When you decided to join the police department, I prayed every day, I said so many novenas, I think I wore out my rosary."

"You have taught me so much, mama. I understand what you mean. My life would have ended too. Vic and I would be empty inside if anything would have happened to Gabriella, so I thank God that everything is almost back to normal. Once this case is finished, I think I'm going to work less and enjoy my daughter more."

"That is the smartest thing you have ever said, but I want to give you some advice if you are willing to listen."

"Of course, mama, what is it?" Raquel asked.

"Gabby may seem fine to you at the moment. She is happy to be back with us, of course. I see she is starting to play and read a little. I even heard her sweet, angelic voice singing before. When we get home, I think you need to take her to talk to someone. Children at that age may have a different idea of life after a trauma that she was forced to endure. Even though it was not very long, it left an impression that she is not able to express," Olga replied.

"I haven't gotten that far in my head, mama. Do you think she will have nightmares or something about the kidnapping?"

"Maybe she will, maybe she won't, but you need to be concerned about the future for your baby. She needs to get this out of her mind."

"I love you so much, mama. I'm so happy you are alive. You will be around for a very long time."

"There is an old expression, daughter. 'Man plans and God laughs.' Everything is in His hands." Olga blessed herself. As did Raquel.

Raquel hugged her mother tightly, her eyes filling up with tears.

"Now go and find that killer. I know you will."

Jimmy Martin and Jack Nagle asked to meet with Vic and Raquel without Fumar and his people.

Just before dinner, they met on the veranda of the White House.

"What's on your mind, boys?" Vic asked.

"We've been working on that cell phone angle you asked us to follow. Looks like it turned out to be a big payoff."

"Early on in the investigation, we were trying to find out if every one of the murdered girls had something missing from their person. With the assumption that the first girl's watch may have been taken, we questioned all of the victims' families and other prostitute friends about the dead girls' watches and jewelry. What we found out is that the victims all had a lot of bracelets, earrings, watches, and rings. Most of it was not of high quality, not worth enough to be fenced. We spun our wheels and came up empty on this," Jack added.

"Cell phones. We know that every victim had a cell phone, right?" Jimmy asked.

"That's a fair assumption," Raquel blurted.

"That's how they communicated with their johns. Generally speaking, either the johns or the pimps called the girls for service. Yet, not one of the victims' cell phones were recovered," Jack added.

"So, your contention is that the killer kept the cell phones as a souvenir. Typical of a serial killer," Raquel declared.

"Yes. We've researched the cell phone providers in Venezuela. There are three main providers. The largest, by far, is Movinet, then Movistar, followed by Digitel. Believe it or not, as poor as that country is at the moment, there are over twenty-six million cell subscribers in Venezuela."

"So, what's your point?" Vic asked.

"It's more than a point, guys. We didn't think that the Vens would be so helpful to an American investigation company, so we worked through INTERPOL. They had to get all the proper paperwork done in Venezuela. That's why it's taken so long. We gave INTERPOL the names of all of the five victims and their home addresses that we found on their passports," Jack offered.

"Go ahead!" Raquel uttered excitedly. Their brains were racing like two horses going toward the finish line.

"So far, we got two hits. Samantha Franco, the first victim, and Pamela Leon, the girl who was found at Punta Espada in the coral cave. INTERPOL worked with Movinet, and these two victims' accounts were found. We were able to get the incoming and outgoing calls on the last day of their lives," Jimmy stated. He was trying hard to fight a smile.

"This is gold!" Vic shouted.

"Just wait!" Jimmy exclaimed.

Jack took over, "There were a lot of calls made before the approximate time of the victims' deaths. All cell-to-cell, mind you. Most of the calls checked out to be the victims' friends, all Venezuelan prostitutes here in the Dominican Republic. Pamela Leon also called her parents in Venezuela. The Franco girl made several calls to Venezuela and to here in the DR. However, we found one phone number that was made to both girls. That number was registered with Orange, one of the major cell providers in the Dominican."

"And?" Raquel asked.

"Lieutenant Castillo got us hooked up, and Orange was very helpful to us," Jimmy answered. "We didn't tell Castillo too much."

"That number, the one that called both girls on the night they were murdered, is registered to CCI, S.A. of Punta Cana," Jack said.

"CCI, S.A.?" Vic asked. He twisted his face a bit as he waited for more intel.

"Cubano Café Internacional. Owned by one Ralph Ledon," Jimmy shouted.

"Areyoukiddenmeorwhat?" Vic screeched.

# CHAPTER 56

Vic called Fumar and asked Lieutenant Castillo and him to return to the White House around eight o'clock that night for a meeting of great importance.

After dinner, when Gabriella was being read a story by her abuelita, Raquel asked Louisa to serve coffee and dessert to Vic, Theresa, and her at the tiki hut.

"Theresa, how ya doin?" Vic asked.

"I'm a wreck inside, if you want the truth," Theresa nearly whispered.

"I bet!" Raquel offered.

"I'm not a very religious person. Maybe I should be after this experience," the tutor admitted.

"There were a lot of prayers for your safety, believe me," Raquel added.

"There is something I want to tell you both. I was more worried for Gabriella than for myself. I swear, I would have given my life for her. Those bastards! How could they? That one guy, the one they called Carlos, he was the sickest of them all. The way he looked at me through that ski-mask thing. And he kept sticking that horrid tongue out. I made sure Gabby never saw that. I kept her back to him all the time. I hope he gets what's coming to him."

"It's time we tell you a few things, Theresa. They all got what was coming to them. Did you or Gabby see anything…anything like the condition of the men when you left?" Raquel queried.

"That's the thing. The man…the older man who saved us, he said 'call me Uncle John.' He covered Gabby's and my head with a blanket when we left. He took it off when we walked to his car. I wanted to run, but he said he was too old to run and there was no need anyway. To answer your question, no, we saw nothing of those horrible men."

"Well, they all got what was coming to them, and then some," Vic blurted.

"They are all dead, Theresa," Raquel added.

"Dead? How?"

"You don't have to know the gory details, but 'uncle John' took care of them."

"Oh…my…God! That nice old man? Who is he really?"

"He's a special man. We have more news for you. That Sergeant Lopez?"

"You mean Manny the creep?" Theresa put her finger near her mouth like she was gagging at the thought of Lopez.

"He's Manny the dead now!" Vic answered.

"WHAT!" Theresa screamed.

"Theresa, we now know why he asked you on a date. Manny masterminded the entire kidnapping. He hired those men, his goal was to kidnap you and Gabby, double-cross those three mutts, and go in guns blazing, killing them, and being the hero cop," Raquel stated.

"Sick…why?"

"To become a national idol so he could rise in the ranks. Maybe in his warped mind, he thought he could get you, too," Raquel added.

"Ya know, now that I think of the day we went around Punta Cana, he was talking politics. More than I cared for, frankly. He said he would one day run for office, maybe be president, and show them all how to run the country. I thought it was just bravado, you know, just bullshit, trying to impress me."

"We are both so sorry you had to go through all this, Theresa. We understand if you would want to leave," Raquel said.

"No way! I love you guys, and I love Gabriella. If I ever have a daughter, that will be her name. Oh…I'm sorry, maybe you want me to leave?"

"Areyoukiddenmeorwhat? No way!" Vic's Bronx came out again.

"Vic…really, enough of that 'kiddin-me-or-what' thing. Hey, let's all go up and tuck that little bugger in," Raquel pronounced.

Fumar, two of his aides, and Lieutenant Castillo arrived promptly at eight o'clock.

Vic hugged the general. "Let's all go outside so we can have a cigar. I still didn't buy any, so I'll have to grubb off you, Fumar," Vic blurted.

"Grubb, that is an English word I've never heard before," Fumar stated.

"Not English. That's Bronx. It means to take stuff from people. Like cigarettes, food, cigars, all sorts of stuff. I'm a grubber right now!"

"I can't get this man out of the Bronx playgrounds, gentlemen," Raquel quipped.

They moved to the veranda, all sitting around the long outdoor table.

"The good thing about cigars, it keeps the bugs away," Fumar joked. His men chuckled politely.

"Gentlemen, we have a new development in the case. We wanted you to hear it quickly, that's why we called this meeting. I'm hoping we can brainstorm and move forward toward a conclusion," Vic announced.

Fumar nodded his head in anxious anticipation.

"I'm not one to take credit for other people's ideas and hard work. Jimmy and Jack will explain," Vic began.

Jimmy and Jack looked at each other, not expecting to be called into the hot seat. Jimmy prodded Jack to start.

"We have tracked down the cell phone records of two out of five of the Venezuelan homicide victims. Through the assistance of INTERPOL and contacts provided by Lieutenant Castillo at Orange, it's been determined that calls were made from a phone owned by Ralph Ledon's company shortly before the girls were murdered," Jack reported.

"Castillo informed me that you were asking for help with Orange. I suspect you verified the findings by checking out the incoming caller?" Fumar asked.

"Yes, sir, we did," Jimmy answered.

"Do you have a list of all cellular phones that are registered to Mr. Ledon's company?"

"Yes, we do. There are twelve cell phones, registered to CCI, S.A.," Jimmy replied again.

"Was the phone that was used to call the two girls in the possession of Mr. Ledon, himself?"

"Not sure, sir. We are not one-hundred percent sure who the user was on those dates, General. The phones could have been shared, for all we know."

"Do we know if Ledon was in Punta Cana the nights when these two victims were called?"

"Not yet, sir." Jimmy replied. Jimmy and Jack were not shaken by the rapid-fire questions from Fumar.

"We know Ledon was in Cuba when the last girl was murdered. We need to find out where he was when the other killings were done," Fumar stated.

"Yes, we do. Look, all roads are leading to Ledon. The coffee in the burlap bags, the Cuban origin of the bags, the tracks from the golf carts, and now the cell calls on a phone registered to his company. It's time we called old Ralphy in," Vic added.

"You know the minute we call Ledon, he will run right to his suit boys in Santo Domingo, and that will be the end of that," Fumar blurted.

"This is the best information and evidence we have on the entire case. I'll deal with Minister Castillo. I'll call him right now, unless you want to deal with his political bullshit."

"Do it, Vic. There is no other way!" Fumar agreed.

# CHAPTER 57

"But Mr. Gonnella, why can't you understand how sensitive things are here?"

"How about we tell that to the families of the victims, Minister Castillo? What about their sensitivity?"

"Ralph Ledon is the wealthiest man in this country. He is capable of changing the outcome of our next election, if not the entire structure of our government. It is beyond ridiculous to say he is a murderer of prostitutes. I cannot allow you to harass a man of Ledon's stature. It's absurd, to say the very least."

"I will repeat myself, sir. I am not accusing Mr. Ledon of murder. We are simply doing what you paid us to do. We are investigating the activity of a serial murderer. The fact that it is indeed a serial killer is a far-gone conclusion. The evidence that we have uncovered is just that, evidence. It is not an indictment."

"I understand the process, Mr. Gonnella; however, you must not rattle Ledon's cage. I will have hell to pay. I am ordering you and General Martinez to stand down," Castillo seethed.

"Fine, Minister, you leave me no choice," Vic baited Castillo.

"No choice? Are you resigning, Mr. Gonnella?"

"Hell no! I never quit. I am about to collect my other five-hundred thousand."

"If this is solely about the money, Mr. Gonnella, we can settle it right now. You can leave at your will, and we will release the money that is in escrow for you."

"That's the biggest payoff I've ever been offered, sir. I've refused money, cars, sex, and kilos of drugs in my career. I never sold myself before, and I'm not falling into your corruption now. So, allow me to show you all of my cards. First, I'm sending my family back home on my own dime. Only because I no longer trust you or anyone else in this shit-hole of a country. Then, I will make a few calls to New York, and this place will be swarming with the news hounds. I know all the producers on Twenty-Twenty, Sixty Minutes, CNN, MSNBC, Fox News, The New York Times, even fucking

Nickelodeon. You see, I've been on their shows many times. Raquel and I are the celebrity detectives everyone loves. These are friends of mine. Talk about tourism? I will do a thing about the danger of bringing your small children to the Dominican Republic and letting your college kids be exposed to a land of corruption, sex, and danger, and the continuation of a serial killer that is running free on this island paradise. I'm sure this is the last thing you fuckers in 'La Capital' want."

"How dare you threaten me, Gonnella!"

"What threat? I didn't make a threat. I never threaten anyone."

# CHAPTER 58

"Mr. Ledon, I'm here for two reasons. The first is to sincerely thank you again for the kindness and generosity you showed to me when my daughter..."

"First off, please, call me Ralph. I told you that the first time we met at our gala. And I will take the liberty of calling you Vic or Victor. As far as my attempt to be of help and solace to you in your time of need, I came to you as a fellow human being. I heard of the terrible event, and I reacted as anyone in my position should."

"You are one of a kind, Ralph."

Vic had taken the chance of going to the Ledon villa alone. Ledon was alone, save for his butler.

"I'm so happy that it all turned out for the best. I've heard that all three of the kidnappers turned up dead. Good! That's where they belong," Ledon exclaimed.

"There were actually four," Vic advised.

"Four?"

"Yes. Sergeant Manuel Lopez."

"What? I know his father quite well."

"I know you do, Ralph. Lopez's father has not yet been told."

"How does one recover from that?"

"I'm sorry to say that Lopez was the mastermind of the kidnapping. Very unfortunate. He had everything to live for, I'm told."

"My God, he certainly did. How did he die?"

"I have no idea. All I know is that he's gone," Vic lied.

"Vic, you said you came for two reasons."

"My second reason, I guess, is in a semi-official capacity."

"Not this murder investigation again, I hope."

"Ralph, I need to explain to you what we've discovered. I know of your contacts with the government here, but I've come here, unannounced, to tell you the evidence is compelling. It seems the killer is, how can I say this delicately? Well, I'm not one to beat around the bush, but I'm not finding the proper words."

"Say what you need to say."

"If the killer is not you, then he is very close to you."

"I can assure you, I've killed no one. I am not your serial killer. At best, I am the lover of Punta Cana," Ledon laughed. "But I'm certain you've heard that declaration from guilty parties before in your career." Ledon was becoming visibly agitated.

"Facts are what brought me here to see you. Perhaps you can help me put the pieces of the puzzle together."

"My attorney advised me not to answer any questions in this regard, but I have nothing to hide personally, so I will ignore his counsel. What facts do you have?"

"All indications are that at least one, perhaps two, of the murdered women were killed here on your property. Blood samples, found on your lawn, match the last victim's DNA. Secondly, the burlap bags had remnants of coffee beans in their fibers. The bags were made in Cuba."

Ledon interrupted, "Killed here at my estate? I'm finding that hard to swallow."

"I can give you the details on our findings. Further evidence ties your personal golf cart tires with the tire tracks left at the place where a victim's body was found."

"I'm not the only one with a golf cart around here. There is a golf cart in almost every villa in and around Punta Espada. Your evidence sounds circumstantial to me."

"Perhaps you are right. But the tires on your vehicle are quite unique. Ignoring any of that evidence, which I believe is enough to make one sit up and take notice, there is a virtual smoking gun that points to you."

Vic continued,"We know you were in Havana the night the last victim was murdered. I would still like to know your whereabouts when the other women were found, but that may not be totally necessary."

"So now, tell me. What is the smoking gun you mentioned?" Ledon asked.

"In the case of two of the homicides, calls were made from a cell phone, registered to your company, directly to the victims. These calls were made on the night of their killings."

Ledon sat back in his chair. His tanned face became slightly drawn.

Vic continued, "Can you see now why I'm here?"

"Registered to my company? I have several cell phones which are used by myself and by others around me. Perhaps one was lost?"

"That's always possible, Ralph. Unfortunately, with the other evidence we have, circumstantial or otherwise, all roads are leading to your doorstep. Can you help with a list of the individuals who have these phones?"

"My lawyer will shoot me, but I am not afraid to tell you. Let me try and remember. The general manager of my plant has a company phone. Our controller, I believe one of our agents here, and one in Havana. Of course, my wife has a phone and so does my butler."

"That's a total of seven phones including your own. I'm told there are a total of twelve phones registered to the company. We will have to match the phone numbers with the user. That shouldn't be too difficult. Unless, as you say, one or more of the remaining five phones are inactive or were lost. There also remains the possibility that a man in your position is being set up. Are you aware of any disgruntled employees at the moment?"

"I guess that's very possible. I like to think I take care of my people well enough so they wouldn't hate me. But one never knows."

"I have another sensitive question, Ralph. And by no means am I judging you. We know that you have a liking for Venezuelan prostitutes. Some of the girls we interviewed attested to that. Do you recall if any of the victims had been with you?"

"I didn't pay close attention to the girls who were murdered. It is indeed possible. I really don't know."

"If I showed you photos of the victims, would that help?"

"Now I'm getting nervous. Maybe I do need to bring my lawyer here."

"That is your prerogative, of course, but you know as well as I that your lawyer will block our investigation. Then I'll get a call from Santo Domingo, and I will be forced to bring the evidence to them. I think we can avoid that very simply."

"How is that?"

"You either admit to being the killer, or help us to find who is," Vic swallowed hard.

"You are a very shrewd man, Vic Gonnella. My entire life, I have done two things that I am very proud of. I have never been afraid to take chances, and I've always lived by my word. There is no written contract that was ever better than my word. I give you my word, with God as my witness, here and now, that I will help you find this so-called Butcher of Punta Cana."

# CHAPTER 59

"Ledon just sent me his itinerary for the past two months. Amazingly, he was out of town for each homicide. Cuba, Brazil, Costa Rica. All on coffee business. He is clearly not our man," Vic announced.

Vic and Raquel were meeting at the White House with Fumar, Lieutenant Castillo, Jimmy, and Jack, along with two of Fumar's aides.

"Unless he's lying," Fumar blurted.

"Honestly, I get a feeling he isn't, but I've been wrong about suspects in the past. Let's see what happens with him."

"Well, he hasn't gone whining to his friends in La Capital. Minister Castillo, in his infinite wisdom, is looking to hang me by the balls, so he would have already called screaming. Excuse my vulgarity, Raquel," Fumar apologized.

"You forget I was an NYPD cop. I've heard a lot worse," Raquel laughed.

"May I state the obvious?" Lieutenant Castillo asked. Fumar shook his head in the affirmative.

"We need to focus on the cell phone users first. Then perhaps track any and all calls going out from all the phones."

"That's a bit difficult. Do you think Orange will cooperate?" Jack asked.

"Not sure, but I can ask," Castillo replied.

Raquel jumped in from left field. "Something just dawned on me! Help me to hear myself think this through. So, in the past month, maybe six weeks, whenever Ralph Ledon was on a trip, a body popped up. Vic, if Ledon really wants to help as he says, either find out if he is going away again or ask him to stage a trip."

"You mean pretend he is going out of town for a few days?" Vic asked.

"Yeah! He lets everyone around him know he's going somewhere. His office, everyone. He hides out in a safe place, and we put a surveillance team on his villa. This way, and it's a stretch, if the killer makes a move, we can be there to nail him."

"That's worth a shot!" Jimmy spewed.

"Do you think he would do it?" Jack asked.

"All I can do is ask," Vis stated.

The meeting broke up about ten o'clock that evening. Vic and Raquel said good night and headed upstairs, Fumar ran outside the main door with his men to light up a cigar and take off to their house, Jimmy and Jack went into the study to watch whatever was on television in English. Lieutenant Castillo spotted Theresa sitting in a high-back, wicker chair alone on the veranda.

"Hello, Theresa."

"Oh, hi, Mateo. How have you been?"

"Am I disturbing you?

"Not at all. Here, please grab a seat. I haven't seen you in days."

Castillo pulled a small, wicker chair away from the table and sat across from Theresa.

"Are you okay?" Castillo asked.

"I'm still getting over it. I'm not sleeping very well. My mind is still replaying that day at the park and all the rest."

"I can understand. I must tell you that I was an absolute, how do you say it in English? Basket, the whole time you and Gabriella were gone."

"You mean a basket case, Mateo. We call it a basket case," Theresa chuckled.

"Oh, yes. That's it! Anyway, the outcome is all that matters. I felt so helpless not being able to help you. Not being a parent, I can only imagine what Vic and Raquel were feeling. And of course, Olga. I thought for sure she…I'm sorry, I'm not helping your mood by replaying the past."

"It's okay, Mateo. I'll be fine. Don't forget, I'm a New York City girl."

"How is it to live and work in that place, New York?"

"Hectic, expensive, crowded…but I like it. Haven't you ever been there?"

"Unhappily, no. I've been to Miami and Washington D.C. but never New York."

"You must visit sometime. There is so much to do. At the moment, I'm just focused on my job with Gabriella, but once I get home, I want to go to a movie and have a pastrami sandwich at Katz."

"Cats? What is that?"

"It's a Jewish delicatessen on the lower east side. Tell you what, Mateo. If you ever come to New York, I'll treat you to Katz's Deli."

"I don't know when I can get away, but I would like that very much."

"It would be nice if we stayed in touch. I'll give you my e-mail address, and we can write from time to time."

"I'm afraid my English writing is quite poor. But I can use Google translator."

"Nothing doing. I can help you with your English writing and reading. I'm a teacher, you know!" Theresa chuckled.

"I would be honored."

"You know, Mateo Castillo, you are a very nice man. I wish I had gone with you to tour Punta Cana instead of…"

"I understand what you are saying. Sadly for me, my shyness stood in my way of asking you. It took me a lot to come over and say hello just now."

"Why so shy, Mateo?"

"Perhaps the manner in which I was raised. To always be a gentleman. Not to be pushy and to let your performance speak for itself."

"Those are good characteristics in a man. You may make someone a great husband one day. And a wonderful father, too."

"Well, thank you for speaking with me. I will leave you to your thoughts, Theresa."

"Mateo, here is your first lesson in tearing down your shyness wall. Please go into the kitchen, get two Presidentes, and come out and drink one with me. Then we will have a second, and then you can go home. And one more thing, if you don't mind. It's driving me crazy. Please open your tie a bit and relax."

# CHAPTER 60

Vic was indeed shrewd as Ralph Ledon said. The former NYPD detective reasoned that if he were to stage Ledon leaving his Punta Cana villa, he very well, innocently or otherwise, could leak the trap to someone close to him. That someone could be the Butcher of Punta Cana.

Vic asked Ledon to meet him at the place where Raquel, Deegan, and he had had dinner, Playa Blanca, on the beach in Punta Cana.

Ledon ordered a bottle of Prosecco and some cheese. The wait staff, seeing the coffee king, hovered over the table until Ledon politely shooed them away.

"You have good taste, Vic. This is my favorite spot in the entire region. Five star all the way," Ledon stated.

"I understand why. Look at this place! And the food is amazing."

"I wouldn't expect you would have the time to get out much, what with the murder investigation and your little girl. How is she doing?"

"Like nothing happened. Kids are resilient. Thank you for asking, Ralph."

"I'm glad to see you but am anxious to hear why you asked me here."

"I wanted to tell you in person that you are not a suspect in this case. Your alibis are waterproof, and your reputation in impeccable. Please accept my apology for any stress we put you through."

"Vic, I eat stress for breakfast, but thank you all the same. Look, you have a job to do. I don't envy your position. Tell me, how is the investigation going?"

"It's a process. Serial killers are generally very bright. They don't signal their next move. I hate to say it, but this guy is likely to strike again, and maybe not in Punta Cana. He's unpredictable. It seems his mission is clear though. It's obvious it has something to do with prostitutes, for some reason they happen to be Venezuelan at the moment, and as you know, they are all over the Dominican. All of the murdered girls have similarities in their looks and approximate age."

"Very strange mission, don't you think?" Ledon asked.

"The reason for the mission won't be known until the killer is captured. History tells us that the end result is the murderer being killed or captured, but in some cases, they stop their spree, making it more difficult to apprehend them," Vic shared.

"This has put a shadow over the region. For one, I hope you find him soon. Another murder may turn Punta Cana into a ghost town."

"Precisely. Have you put any more thought into any disgruntled employees or competitors?"

"Of course I have. I've racked my brain. I came up with nothing to help you. Other than the jealousy of a random person, I really have no enemies. At least none that I know of."

"I wish it were that easy, Ralph."

"Forgive me, but I want to get back to something you said before. You know of my history. An orphan, left alone when my parents were killed by the communists in Cuba. That fact has always haunted me, Vic. My entire life, through all of my success, I always felt something was missing. Perhaps my parents and the rest of my family who were lost to me. When you said children are resilient, I had to pause to wonder how resistant to trauma children really are. I see this all the time in the orphanage I established here. The kids all seem happy on the surface, but there is something deep down that reminds me of my own despair. I am not one to give advice freely, especially to people I hardly know." Ledon stopped and stared out onto the water.

"Go ahead Ralph, please."

"Your daughter lives a wonderful life which you and your lady have provided. Please, take every effort to ensure what happened to her doesn't haunt her later in life."

Vic was nonplussed and thought, *How can this man, as rich and powerful as he is, be so sensitive?*

After a pregnant pause, Vic replied.

"This is the same advice that Raquel's mother gave her. Thank you for your sincere concern, Ralph. You know, I had a severe trauma in my life when I was just about my daughter's age. It lingered with me my entire life. If it weren't for Raquel, I don't know what would have happened to me. I'm embarrassed to say I never thought of what you are saying. I should have known better. You are truly a great man."

"So now you have a great man's two cents."

Ledon continued, "Let me ask you, Victor, all of that evidence that surrounded me, what do you make of all that? Especially the telephones. Do you still think someone who I know is the killer?"

"Yes, I do…well someone who knows you or who is brilliant enough to set you up with circumstantial evidence. Right now, we are looking at all possibilities. There is also a possibility that we may never catch this guy. Remember Jack the Ripper? Never caught."

Ralph continued, "Makes for good mystery books, doesn't it Vic? Listen, I am going to Columbia tomorrow to look at a coffee plant. I'll be gone for a few days. I hope when I return, you will have captured this maniac."

# CHAPTER 61

"We have a day to set up a surveillance on the Ledon villa. Ledon told me he is leaving on a business trip to Columbia. Do you think we can get lucky?" Vic asked.

"Do you know what time he is leaving for Columbia and for how long?" Raquel inquired.

"All I know is that he is going to Columbia for a few days. That's all Ledon said, and I didn't want to push it."

"And tomorrow is Friday. The timing seems too perfect," Jimmy said.

"He seems to usually go away toward the end of the week. Maybe he has a lady friend?" Lieutenant Castillo added.

"That's his business. Now we need to concentrate on trapping the killer," Vic spouted.

"What's the plan?" Raquel asked.

"Lieutenant, can you put the aerial photo of Punta Espada on the whiteboard? I need a view of the Ledon villa," Vic asked.

Castillo moved quickly. Using a laptop, he brought the Ledon villa, the surrounding area, and the nearby golf hole into focus.

Vic used a pointer to make his plan. "Let's put our heads together. Look, we can't spook this guy. No cars anywhere near the villa. Jimmy, I want you to go across the Punta Espada fairway across from the villa. Up here on this hill, Fumar, do you have a high-powered telescope? One that Jimmy can see what's going on outside the house?"

"I will have one here in the morning from the army," Fumar replied.

"Good, so Jimmy, we will all be communicating on the wireless. Jack, you did camouflage surveillance in the Marines, correct?"

"Yes, sir."

"You will be stationed in the back of the villa. Somewhere near that fish pool. There is plenty of foliage for you to blend in. Fumar, add some infrared goggles and a couple of camouflage outfits for Jimmy and Jack to your shopping list, please."

"Done!" Fumar exclaimed.

"Fumar, you, Castillo, and your men, commandeer some of those friggin' golf carts from Punta Espada. You will stand ready below the house and out of sight, hugging this hill on the golf course. Freddy said they lock up the carts when the last golfers finish playing. That should be just around dusk. Follow instructions from Jimmy and Jack if and when they say go."

"No problem."

"Raquel and I will station ourselves nearby. One of those villas near the Ledon house should be empty. We will be there with our ears on."

"Vic, we don't know if the killer brings the girl inside the villa or not. If it's inside, I may not have eyes on them," Jack stated.

"Excellent point. If the girl goes inside the house, Jimmy, you need to tell us. Raquel and I will go to the front of the villa and try to see inside. If the killer takes the girl outside to do his thing, Jack…you take him out at the first sign of anything. Got it?"

"Yes, sir! No problem!" Jack replied.

"Best case, we try to take him alive. Just don't sacrifice the victim," Vic declared.

"And no one outside the people in this room should know of this operation," Raquel added.

"Correct. This may or may not be a good chance for us. We will all assume and behave as if a murder will be going down in or around that villa tomorrow night," Vic declared.

"Fumar, are we missing anything, General?"

Fumar took his unlit Churchill from between his lips.

"Let's go over this a few times. I think we can accomplish this operation with precision. I want to add one more thing. I will have a couple of my men at the airport. Just to make sure Ledon is indeed getting on his jet."

# CHAPTER 62

Friday morning was not the usual fabulous weather for which Punta Cana is known. The skies were threatening, with billowing, dark rain clouds and no shining sun even trying to peek through. The temperature dropped into the mid-seventies, with the feel and smell of imminent rain.

Vic and Raquel were lying in bed waiting for the alarm clock to buzz. They couldn't sleep, thinking about the Ledon villa operation, going over and over the plans in their minds. After two rounds of steamy sex, the couple finally got a few hours sleep.

"The forecast isn't great today, even though the weather channel on my phone says its eighty-four and sunny," Raquel noted.

"More bullshit. Look toward the money. Someone is paying off someone to make paradise a little more heavenly than it actually is. It's going to open up soon and rain all day. The no-bullshit weather channel is calling for severe thunderstorms this afternoon into tonight," Vic added.

"How will that affect the operation?"

"It may chase the killer, but as far as we go, all it will do is get us a bit wet. I hope Fumar thinks about bringing rain gear for us. Especially Jimmy and Jack."

"Want to call him?"

"I was thinking about it, but I don't want to sound like I think he's totally incompetent. I'm sure this case has twisted his balls a bit. Especially with that freehold Minister Castillo up his ass every time something happens."

"Let me ask you something that I just can't understand. Not only in this country but all over. So, Minister Castillo is from this wealthy sugar cane family. Just like the Kennedys, their father was a rich guy, too. The Rockefellers, so many wealthy people who can just keep making big money and live in the lap of luxury for generation upon generation. Why do these guys get into politics?"

"Very simple, honey. More money and power. They pretend to want to help their people, their country, society, but it's all a crock of shit," Vic lectured.

"It's gonna be a long day, just waiting around for dark? Did anyone ever think he would kill a girl during the day?" Raquel asked.

"Great question. The time of death on all the girls indicated they were choked out either late at night or just after midnight. I think we just keep with the history here."

Vic continued, "Anyway, Fumar and everyone will be here at noon. Louisa will make a nice lunch. Mama, Gabriella, and Theresa will go stir crazy, Fumar will smoke twelve cigars, and I will go bat shit crazy worrying about tonight."

"Move over, I'll be right there with you."

Fumar and his men came loaded for bear. Except there aren't any bears in the Dominican Republic. Perhaps it should be said that they were loaded for iguana.

A Dominican Republic Army HMMWV utility vehicle was appropriated by Fumar without the general having to explain why he needed the vehicle. Larger than a normal commercial van, the green army truck was full of various gear that Fumar borrowed.

Camouflage uniforms, the ones that Vic had asked for Jimmy and Jack, including floppy military hats, rain wear, boots, and all the trimmings, would be worn by Fumar and his men as well. Infrared goggles, enough for the entire staff, were charged up and ready for action. A Tikka T3 Beretta bolt action sniper rifle was requisitioned for Jack Nagle. Fumar missed nothing and left nothing to chance.

"After lunch, we all will go through the equipment. I advise that your daughter, her teacher, and her abuelita be sequestered to the upstairs rooms. There is no reason to frighten them," Fumar ordered.

"Thank you, General, they have been through enough," Raquel replied.

Louisa outdid herself with her classic arroz con pollo, chicken and rice, for everyone, complete with a family-style salad and a huge tres leches milk cake. The coffee pot was percolating non-stop, as it would be for the rest of the day.

Batista, the house boy, was given the day off with pay. There was no reason for the young man to be there to pose a potential leak issue.

The clock seemed as if it would be dragging until the time to deploy the operation, which was set for dusk. Every one of Fumar's men had military experience and were well trained in field operations. Jimmy Martin wasn't in the army back home, but being stationed with Vic in the NYPD's 41st precinct in the Bronx, also known as Fort Apache back in the day, was more than enough military-like experience.

Fumar's cell phone chimed. The general looked at the phone, made a smirk, and pressed the red button, rejecting the call. He called Lieutenant Castillo to the side.

"That call was from your…I'm sorry, from Castillo. I'm not taking any of his calls until tonight's maneuver is complete. He will call the phone here now. Don't answer," Fumar ordered.

"With pleasure, sir,"

Like clockwork, the war room phone rang and rang until the caller gave up.

A minute later, Fumar's phone rang again. He looked at the phone angrily, expecting it to be Minister Castillo. He accepted this one.

"Yes, go ahead."

"General, Ralph Ledon just arrived at the airport. He is about to board the plane," his man advised.

"Good. Wait there until you see it take off. Then text me," Fumar commanded.

"Everyone, it's confirmed Ledon is indeed leaving. He is boarding his plane at this moment," Fumar announced.

Vic made a nervous laugh. "There was always the possibility that I was wrong and he is the Butcher. I'm glad he's gone."

Fumar chimed in. "You are assuming there will be a murder tonight, Vic."

"I feel it in my bones," Vic chuckled.

"I will be totally convinced when we capture the killer," Raquel whispered.

"It's zero three hundred. Let's get moving. Lieutenant, have your men bring the equipment from the vehicle," Fumar ordered.

# CHAPTER 63

With Ralph Ledon now likely in Cartagena, Vic, Raquel, and Fumar, along with the rest of the group, moved toward the staging area and final instructions. Everyone met in the parking lot of Punta Espada golf club. The steady rain and the brisk wind which came off the sea made for difficult visibility and considerable discomfort to all those assembled.

Fumar stood up in the open passenger side of the utility vehicle. The general looked over his troops with a stern, yet dignified, expression. "Gentlemen and lady, we have gone over our assignments in great detail. Remember, if there is a woman brought to the villa by the perpetrator, we in no way want to jeopardize her life simply to catch this killer. Jack, your orders are clear. Do not hesitate."

"Yes, sir!" Jack bellowed.

"Now, I would like us all to bow our heads for a moment of silence for the women who were murdered here, and ask whomever you pray to for a just resolution to this case," Fumar added.

Vic kept silent, allowing the general to lead the operation.

"The sky will darken in a few minutes. Do the best you can with the rain and wind. Watch for my signal to move out."

Jack Nagel and Jimmy Martin were taken in golf carts by Fumar's officers, using the natural terrain of the golf course to mask their movements.

Jimmy kept his head down as he made his way toward the vantage point across the fairway and the Ledon villa. He was hoping for a clear view of the interior of the villa, but the weather prevented all but what looked like flickering lights from the home. He was hoping the rain would let up to make his location viable.

Jack's training kicked into high gear as he belly-crawled through the wet sand and soil from the rear of the Ledon villa. Jack hid in a tangle of bushes, shooing a few non-venomous snakes and chasing a dark solenodon, a venomous, shrew-like creature with a long nose, back into its burrow. The former Marine sat Indian style, his legs crossed comfortably. He removed the sniper rifle from its sheath, keeping the barrel safely pointed to the ground. From his vantage point near the teaming fish pool,

Jack had a full view of the entire backyard. Two high-intensity, outdoor lamps illuminated the swimming pool and rear of the villa.

Fumar and his men were tucked away out of sight on the side of the sandy hill beneath the villa. Twenty of the general's men were in five golf carts that were commandeered from the Punta Espada vehicle barn.

Raquel and Vic sat in the black Cadillac Escalade under a canopy in the driveway of a vacant villa about a hundred yards south of the Ledon Villa.

Darkness had set in as everyone hunkered down in their strategic positions.

"I have movement! Jimmy blurted through his wireless, "Can't really see too much, but there is a figure leaving through the front door of the villa. Could be a male."

Silence followed for a few seconds.

"It is a male. He's carrying a bag of some kind. Like a gym bag, like that. He's getting into a vehicle that is parked inside of the garage. Can't make it out from here…it's a sedan. Looks grey or green. Sorry, can't really tell," Jimmy followed.

"If he comes past our position, we'll try to make him," Vic stated.

The wireless clicked back on, "It's the butler. Let's see if he returns," Vic announced.

"Is there any movement inside the house?" Fumar asked.

"Can't see inside," Jimmy responded.

"Negative. No movement," Jack replied.

Everyone waited. The time was nine-ten.

At ten o'clock, the wireless chirped.

"Light went on upstairs. The drapes are drawn. Could be a bedroom," Jack observed.

The rain began to let up. Cascades of lightning out at sea was brightening the distant night sky.

They waited.

"I just got a flashback from when I was a cop. We had information on a drug buy on Castle Hill Avenue. We waited in an unmarked all night. Nothing happened," Raquel uttered to Vic.

"Let's hope our theory brings more than nothing," Vic replied.

"I have to pee!"

"You have two choices. Hold it in or squat in those bushes," Vic laughed.

"Yeah, right. Too many crawly things. I'll hold it…for a while."

"Upstairs light went off. Could be bedtime," Jack announced.

Fumar tapped in. "Watch all the exits," the general warned.

A minute later, Jimmy chimed in, "The garage door just opened. Stay with me. It's a bit clearer from here. A car is pulling out, red lights and a backup light. It's an SUV. Can't make out the driver."

"Hopefully the car will come by us," Vic stated.

"No luck there. The vehicle went north. Toward the water and the club house, it looks like." Jimmy said.

"SHIT!" Vic blurted.

"Everyone stay in your positions. Now we wait," Fumar ordered.

The radio was silent for thirty minutes.

"I have to pee bad," Raquel declared.

"Just open the door and pee, for Christ's sake. It's not like I haven't seen you pee before."

"Asshole!"

Raquel undid her camouflage pants and slipped out of the Escalade. She closed the passenger door to kill the light. She finished and jumped back into the vehicle.

"Nice ass!" Vic said.

"Double asshole!"

Jimmy broke the radio silence, "Car coming from the north. Looks like that SUV."

"I guess it ain't the butler!" Raquel whispered to Vic.

Everyone held their breath.

"SUV pulling into the driveway. I can see two heads, but I can't make… vehicle is pulling into the garage. Door is going down. Couldn't make out occupants."

"Two heads? You sure, Jimmy?" Vic asked.

"Affirmative. That's all I could make out," Jimmy confirmed.

Vic went into high gear. "Jack, watch closely. Can you move up without being seen?"

"Roger that. I can crawl up a bit, nearer to the swimming pool. Hold it. A few lights went on…ground floor. I see shadows moving. That's all."

"Okay, get as close as possible. We are moving on foot to the front of the house. We will try to put eyes inside.

"I'm glad you peed. Let's move it!"

Vic and Raquel jogged toward the front of the Ledon villa. When they arrived, Vic pointed toward the ground where some decorative pebbles and crushed coral surrounded the entrance to the driveway. He and Raquel jumped over the stones.

They moved silently toward the windows in the front of the villa. Vic toward the right side of the door, Raquel toward the left. Suddenly, two bright lights beamed down, illuminating the front of the house.

"FUCK! Sensors!" Raquel whispered.

Vic and Raquel froze among the bushes near the front windows. They held their breath, waiting for an exterior light over the front door to go on.

Nothing.

The couple could hear soft, Latin music coming from inside. A woman laughed.

Vic peered into the great room. The lights were down low, but he could make out the two inhabitants. They were kissing.

"I'll be dipped in shit!" Vic blurted softly. He waved for Raquel to join him.

Raquel moved slowly, the lights in the front yard were still blaring.

"Take a look!"

"Holy shit. I can't fucking believe it!" Raquel uttered.

"Hey, let's not assume anything. The husband is away. Maybe he's not ringing her bell anymore," Vic said.

Raquel looked closer. "Wait a second. Look at the table. Looks like cut up pieces of coconut. A bottle of rum, Vic, it's the killer. What the hell, the…"

"Everyone move in, Jack…go inside…now!" Vic announced on the wireless.

Vic and Raquel hit the front door a couple times, finally smashing through the lock.

Jack was first inside. A young woman, dressed in a tight, one-piece, flesh-colored jumpsuit, her high heels on the floor, was passed out on a divan. Jack raised his rifle, tucking it hard into his right shoulder.

"Drop that thing, or I take your fucking head off right here…DO IT!" Jack shouted.

Vic grabbed the killer from behind, pulling a wire garrote from her hand. Lissandra Hoyos-Ledon silently stared down at the drugged girl on the sofa.

# CHAPTER 64

Fumar and his men barged into the villa, fanning out in every direction, firearms drawn. Lieutenant Castillo ran toward Vic and Ledon's wife. The young officer couldn't believe his eyes. Lissandra was dressed in a long, skin-tight, lavender dress, with a split that went from her ankles to just below her crotch. She resembled a runway model, her dark brown hair pulled back into a tight bun, accentuating her high cheekbones.

Jimmy Martin arrived at the villa. "What the fuck?" was the best he could garner at seeing Lissandra and the unconscious girl.

Vic did not speak. He sat down in a winged, leather chair. Vic looked around the magnificent, opulent villa, flashing back to his parents' one-bedroom apartment when he was a child in the Bronx. He thought about what had happened to his daughter. He thought about John Deegan. He began to tremble.

Lissandra finally broke from her trancelike state. "I guess you want to ask me why?" she said to no one in particular.

"Mrs. Ledon. Your silence is probably in your best interest," Fumar offered.

"What can they do to me beyond the rest of my life in prison? There is no death penalty here. I will live until I want to die. I've been mentally tortured inside this prison. Take a look at me. Is this not enough? I see how men look at me. Ever since I was a little girl, I could see how men wanted me," Lissandra screamed.

"Calm down please, try to be silent," Fumar repeated.

"I killed those girls, all of them, to rid this world of these pigs. My husband demanded I do disgusting things with him and these fucking women. I made them all believe I wanted them. Their greed is what killed them in the end. I took their numbers from his phone while that dog slept," Lissandra seethed.

Castillo cuffed Lissandra's hands behind her back.

"You gave up your life and your freedom to do this?" Raquel asked as she moved closer to the crazed woman.

"My life was shit. I wanted a baby. He said no. I wanted to leave him, he threatened to kill me. Now I will laugh in his face. Think of his embarrassment. The wife of one of the richest men in the Caribbean is the Butcher of Punta Cana!" Lissandra laughed hysterically. She kept laughing until she broke down into a screaming cry.

"Captain Castillo, take her to the hospital until I give further orders. Make sure she is well guarded, nobody is to see her," Fumar commanded.

"Yes, sir, but you called me Captain."

"That's correct. You are now a captain. Any complaints?"

"No, sir. Thank you, sir."

"It's the least I can do to aggravate that fucking minister."

# CHAPTER 65

Gabriella was fast asleep just fifteen minutes after takeoff from Punta Cana International.

Gabby was sitting next to Theresa, with her abuelita right across the aisle. Olga, fingering her rosary beads, her lips moving rapidly with each prayer in thanks to her Lord for sparing her only grandchild.

Theresa got up to use the ladies' room and stopped to chat with Vic and Raquel.

"Just before we left, Captain Castillo thanked us all for helping with the case. He's such a sweet man," Theresa stated.

"He must be happy with his promotion," Raquel added.

"He is. He also got a two-week vacation as a bonus. He's planning on coming to New York for a visit."

"That's great, it would be great to see him. We can give him the grand tour," Vic offered.

Theresa gave a shy smile.

"Oh, I get it! He wants to see you," Vic blurted.

"That would be so much fun!" Raquel added.

"I offered for him to stay at my place. I have two bedrooms. Want to hear his response?"

"Sure," Raquel said.

"He said it would be an imposition, and he didn't think it would be appropriate. Can you imagine?"

"Awww, he's a real gentleman," Raquel praised.

"Theresa, where I come from, that's called a keeper," Vic laughed.

"Ya never know!" Theresa uttered. The teacher returned to her seat and her sleeping student.

"I got a call from Minister Castillo just before we left. I wanted to wait to tell you the good news," Vic whispered to his lady.

"Let me guess, he's releasing the other five hundred thou," Raquel blurted.

"Good guess."

"No guess. They were thrilled that we were able to stop the insanity. God knows how many more poor girls she would have murdered."

"I thought for sure it was Ralph Ledon. Until he started playing ball with us, I would have bet the entire fee it was him. Everything pointed to him. His penchant for Venezuelan hookers, the burlap bags, the evidence on his golf cart, the blood in his backyard. Just goes to show you...never assume anything," Vic uttered.

"Did Lissandra say why she covered the girls' heads with the coffee bags?" Raquel asked.

"Fumar told me she was asked that question, and she babbled about something to do with insulting Ralph's millions."

"Psychologists will write about the coffee bags for years. She has a classic serial killer mentality. Turns out she was molested as a little girl by a cousin and an uncle. Her father was a drunk, and the mother may have traded sex for food. That's what she alluded to anyway, according to Fumar," Raquel offered.

"Not to mention she kept all the victims' cell phones as souvenirs. And the watch from the first murder. They were found hidden in her panty draw. Talk about symbolism!"

"I never thought it was Ralph. To me, it was a tossup between Freddy and that creepy Lenny, but Freddy had me going for a while. Taking the girl to the golf course at night and threatening to kill her turned my blood cold."

"When Jack found that chloral hydrate in that weirdo Dr. Fishman's office, I thought we had him nailed," Vic mentioned.

"That guy was so friggin' creepy. To think he touched my boob makes me want to vomit."

"You have to admit, honey, Fishman has good taste when it comes to boobs," Vic chuckled."

"I see. Are you turned on by that kind of shit, Gonnella? Yuck! What's going to happen to him, anyway?"

"Fumar let him go. Costa Rica. He'll start all over again."

"And Lenny?"

"Don't really know, but I have a feeling that he didn't miss a beat. Guys like him always seem to survive."

"Hey, Deegan, what about Deegan?" Raquel asked.

"Before, I forgot to tell you. The day after we captured Lissandra, after all the excitement and all the silly calls from Santo Domingo and the party we had that afternoon, Fumar and I walked our cigars up to the beach. You will never guess what Fumar said to me," Vic muttered.

"He had the hots for my mama?"

"Geez, will you be serious. He told me he finally figured out who Deegan was. He went back and researched us on the internet and saw a photo of John. You know the one, when he was chairman of his company, in the suit and tie. He's older and thinner now, but the mug is basically the same."

"What did he say?"

"He knew it was him, and he knew of the bounty on Deegan's head, but he thought if Deegan was around us, we had a very good reason. Can you imagine?"

"And to think I didn't like him at first," Raquel replied.

"Let's see. It's like four o'clock in the afternoon in Switzerland. Let's call our favorite serial killer. Our phone won't work up here, but let's see if the pilot has one of those special analog phones."

Sure enough, the Dominican Republic had older phones on their plane.

"Well, hello, Mr. Deegan," Raquel said.

"Perfect timing! Gjuliana just went to the fishmonger, and I'm having a nice Campari and soda. Very European, you know," John replied.

"I guess you heard the news by now."

"What's that…Trump had an affair with Hillary?" John chuckled.

"No, silly man. The Butcher of Punta Cana was caught. We did it, John! Hold on, Vic wants to say hello."

"And you helped us tremendously. We can't thank you enough for all you've done, John."

"Let me guess…it was the wife, right?" Deegan asked.

"Stop the bullshit, where did you hear the news?"

"Swear to God. I have no idea."

"Last I knew, you didn't believe in God."

"Never said that. It's the church I loathe. Okay, I swear on Gjuliana."

"Now I know you're serious. How did you guess it was Lissandra and not Ralph Ledon?"

"Never a guess, Gonnella. You needed to take a closer look at her first off. Not at all the sexy equipment she carries. You had to look into her eyes. I spent quite some time with her pretending to be that photographer. The woman had the eyes of a killer. Like mine. There is a certain look all killers have, an emptiness, a thousand-yard stare, I think it's been called. That prick of a butler was a pussy. The husband, I figured him for a degenerate, but no way is he a killer. So, using geometric logic, whatever that is, I deduced it was Lissandra."

"So, it begs the question, why didn't you tell us?"

"Even a bird knows when to let the chicks fly on their own."

"What? What about a bird?"

"Kiss Gabriella for me," Deegan said. As is his want, Deegan cut the call.

Vic turned to Raquel with a quizzical look. "He knew all along. He friggin' knew!"

Before Raquel could reply, the quiet of the jet was suddenly disrupted by a scream from Gabriella. Everyone jumped at the sound of the distressed child. She was awakened by a nightmare.

"Mommy, daddy, mommy, help me, help me, mommy!"

Naturally, Raquel was the first to comfort her daughter, picking Gabby up from her seat and hugging her. Raquel gently shook her daughter awake.

"There, Gabby, it's okay, mommy is here with you."

Gabby sobbed for a few minutes until she fully woke from the bad dream.

"And look, your abuelita and daddy and Ms. Panny…we are all here for you."

"I saw those men in the masks. They were chasing me and chasing me. And then Uncle John was there and they took one look at him and they all ran away."

"Ay, Dios mío," Olga said, blessing herself three times.

Raquel looked at her mother quickly and sat down with Gabby. Raquel knew her mother was right. "Okay, my love, those men will never harm you. Never!"

"Okay, mommy…but will we ever see Uncle John again?" Gabby asked. She was still trying to catch her breath.

"Yes, we will make absolutely sure we see Uncle John again."